It's like this book was wri[tten] a new start-up, it is over the different facets of ma perfect level of detail to r...., ...

customer acquisition strategies for your business and provides a great approach on how to think about scaling your business. Highly recommended for all entrepreneurs!

—Kristin Langenfeld
CEO, Good Buy Gear

I wish I had this book when I started my career. It would have saved me 10 years of trials and errors. It's a must-read for anyone starting in digital marketing.

—Pierre Lechelle
SaaS Growth Marketer

How to Acquire Your First Million Customers *is both inspirational and practical. This book is a resource that people can turn to again and again. When you are just starting out with a new business, the book serves as a roadmap for digital marketing. As you progress, you will see that the book is worth returning to for its layer upon layer of insights and tips.*

—Laura Kornish
Marketing Division Chair, Leeds School of Business,
University of Colorado Boulder

We came from a coaching background when we started our company, The Coaches Site, and learning how to grow an online business on the fly was a challenge. We discovered we needed to learn a whole new language. How to Acquire your First Million Customers *provides readers with a blueprint to jumpstart their online business and develop a proven process for discovering its true potential. It's a must-read for anyone in the early stages of starting up and will sharpen the skill set of those who have already gained momentum online.*

—Aaron Wilbur
Founder of The Coaches Site

Using their knack for marketing and business lingo paraphrasing, Ken and Chris give wildly practical examples and actionable strategies for growing a customer base. I'm confident this book will inspire readers in the same way Ken inspired me as my first acquisition-focused manager.

—Jenny Hadden
Global Head of Marketing Analytics, Xero

How To Acquire Your First Million Customers

Ken McDonald and Chris Newton

Contents

About the Authors / 7

Prologue / 9

Part I: Laying the Foundation for Growth / 12

Working Backward / 13

Is Your Speedometer Working? / 19

Capitalize on What You Know Already / 25

Are You Ready? / 30

ROAS: The Holy Grail—Spend Less than You Earn / 32

Part II: Customer Acquisition Strategies / 35

Friends and Family / 36

Paid Search / 39

SEO / 46

Social Media / 56

Video / 61

Partnerships / 67

Influencer Marketing / 70

Press Relations (PR)—Getting the Attention of the
      Media / 73

Affiliate Marketing / 80

Customer Referral Programs—Getting Your Customers
      to Spread the Word / 83

Virality—The Age of the Cat Video / 85

Podcasts / 90

Offline—Yeah, It Can Still Work / 92

Content Marketing / 97

Part III: Maximizing Your Traffic (Squeeze as Much Juice as You Can) / 101

AB Testing Makes Everything Better / 104
Micro Tweaks—Going Deeper / 110
Email Marketing / 112
Retargeting / Remarketing / 118

Part IV: Operating the Machine / 121

There Is No Silver Bullet / 122
Assembling Your Winning Customer Acquisition Team / 127

Part V: Tools & Technical Considerations / 133

A Note on Google Analytics / 134
A Plug for Tag Management—Making You More Efficient / 136
Don't Get Too Focused on the Last Click—A Word on Attribution Tracking / 140
Picking the Best Tools for You / 143
Big Finish / 144

About the Authors

Ken McDonald

Ken has been involved with customer growth for the better part of 25 years. For example, starting in 1998, he was a leader on Oracle's e-commerce team. There he helped grow Oracle's e-commerce business from a relatively small site to one that was doing hundreds of millions of dollars a year in business. At the time, it was one of the largest e-commerce sites on the web.

Later Ken joined LifePics, an online photo company, where he ran everything from marketing to product management to account management. While Ken was there, he grew LifePics from a few thousand users to a user base of over 12 million.

After LifePics, Ken joined TeamSnap as Chief Growth Officer. At TeamSnap he runs growth marketing, sales, analytics, and ad sales. During his tenure at TeamSnap, he has used cutting-edge analytics to grow TeamSnap from half a million users to 15 million users. He also drove the B2B side of TeamSnap's business from a handful of users to roughly 3,000 customers.

You can reach Ken on Twitter at @kenpmcdonald

Chris Newton

Chris has been a thought leader and innovator in the digital marketing space since the early 2000s. He wrote and published two books on Microsoft Project and Microsoft Project Server while working for QuantumPM. Shortly after, Ken McDonald hired Chris to come work at LifePics. Under Ken's leadership, Chris learned the ins and outs of digital marketing, serving as Director of Online Marketing for the company during the final years of his tenure.

More recently, Chris has led marketing and e-commerce efforts working for both Hilton and Marriott International, overseeing a portfolio of high-profile hotels and resorts, and managing multi-million dollar marketing budgets in major markets such as San Francisco, Denver, New York City, Chicago, and Hawaii.

Prologue

LET'S START BY SAYING this: We are not going to call you a millennial. Or master blender. Or curator. Or multitasker. Or any other overused buzzword that pigeonholes you into a category you didn't ask to be in. Nope. So let's say this instead: Congratulations on being someone with an idea. After all, ideas are hard. Turning those ideas into a business is even harder. Turning that business into a success (whatever your definition of "success" is) is harder still. But, don't worry. We're here to help.

We wrote this book for anyone looking to better understand how to grow your online business and acquire customers, particularly through digital marketing. You might be a founder of a start-up company, a student, a seasoned vet looking to learn more about this space, a technical person hoping to better understand relationships between digital channels and customers, an executive searching for new ways to achieve revenue growth, or someone else entirely. If you've gotten this far, there is a good chance you have an interest in tactics to grow online businesses. If so, this book is for you.

The foundation of just about any business is customers. You need to acquire customers, retain customers, convert customers, convince customers to perform an action, and so on. That is what we are going to focus on in this book. You've seen the title, so you have some idea of what you're about to read. We promise to discuss our topics in a way that is relatable, approachable, conversational, and hopefully, easy to understand and implement into your day-to-day.

We should stop here for a brief moment to introduce ourselves. We have a combined 25-plus years of online marketing experience at the time of this writing, working in a wide range of environments: start-ups with shoestring budgets to Fortune 500 companies with millions to spend on digital marketing, and everything in between. The companies we've worked for have experienced explosive growth, in several cases reaching over 10 million customers in a short period of time. We also have advised companies that floundered because they failed to follow the best practices of online customer acquisition.

In this book we will walk you through the basics of how to scale your online business. People always ask us for the silver bullet that will help them reach their first million customers, but the reality is that growing your customer base is about following some core principles — and having the discipline to stick to them. If you follow these best practices, you will scale your business, or quickly come to understand where the bottlenecks are. If those bottlenecks cannot be overcome, you generally will figure that out before you lose too much hair (and time, and money) in the process.

It's also worth noting that we'll cover many of the techniques in this book at a high level, but we won't include all the workarounds, nuances, and other details. If we did that, the book would simply be too long. Also, due to the constantly changing nature of online tools and analytics systems, our solutions would quickly become obsolete.

So, let's start with the myth that it is all about the product. If you have a great site or app, everyone will flock to it and you won't need to do any marketing. Right? No. It is true that a great site or app is incredibly helpful. You cannot sell what people don't want. Having said that, with the millions of apps and sites that exist in the world today, it is incredibly hard to be discovered. You almost always have to do some marketing to launch the company. Even if the product is highly viral, you still need to manage that virality. It doesn't happen on its own.

With that … let's get into it.

Part I: Laying the Foundation for Growth

BUILDING A HOUSE IS a wildly overused metaphor for describing various business processes. It goes something like this: Before you can put up the walls (a metaphor for defining your business model), install the roof (a metaphor for completing your project), or move in (a metaphor for reaping the benefits of your hard work), you've got to lay the foundation. In other words, if you don't start properly, the rest of your efforts will likely fall apart. But there is a reason that this metaphor is such a cliché. Why? Because ... wait for it ... it's true!

Customer acquisition strategies are fun to talk about, and believe us, there is a lot on that coming up in this book. But you really need to first understand how to set yourself up for success. Going back to the house, you need to review your plans, survey the land, get the right tools in place, and so on. You get the idea. Let's ditch this metaphor and get into what this all means.

Working Backward

When companies launch, all too often they kick off a blizzard of marketing activities without thinking through what they are trying to achieve. If you were headed somewhere you have never been, would you just get in your car and start driving without thinking about how you are going to get there (or without firing up Google Maps)? Of course not! The same applies here.

What are you trying to achieve? For a lot of companies that are just launching, they will be looking toward financing from angel or venture capital investors. Hopefully you will have started discussions with those investors and have a feel for what it would take for them to invest. Some will look toward customer milestones. If you have an ad-driven model, the milestone will often be around hitting a minimum number of daily active users (DAUs).

DAUs — Daily Active Users

DAUs represent how many distinct people use your site on a daily basis. This is a great measure of how many engaged users you have. If a site or app requires users to log in to access most of the functionality, it will typically associate DAUs with how many users logged in each day. In other words, a user doesn't count if they don't log in, and if they log in from a couple of devices, they still only count once.

If you have a freemium model, investors might want to see a certain number of paying users. In an e-commerce business, the metric might be hitting a certain number of customers who have placed an order with your site.

Freemium Business Model

A freemium business model is one where you allow users to sign up and use the service for free, then encourage them to migrate to a paid plan over time. For example, many online radio or streaming sites offer a freemium model with the option to upgrade to a paid model in exchange for more features. Sometimes, a freemium model will include a trial of all the paid features. The key to these business models is finding the right product structure to entice customers to find value in upgrading to the paid plans.

Alternately, the metrics can be very financial in nature. Revenue targets are usually straightforward: Hit $X per year in revenues. Or, they can be around profitability: Show us that X% of your freemium customers will pay, or that your acquisition costs will be less than what customers spend with you. If you are trying to run the company without investors, profitability is key.

Another set of goals might be geographic in nature. For example, the goal could be to acquire at least 10% of the potential customers in at least two cities. This kind of geographic goal is very popular in two-sided marketplaces (business models with two distinct sets of user groups, such as patients and doctors for health insurance providers) and other businesses that have a strong local component. Craigslist is a great example of an online site with a strong local component. Investors might say that they want to see the company be successful in a certain geographic area before they give the company more financial backing to test the concept much more broadly.

All things being equal, we particularly like revenue goals because revenue pays the bills. You cannot pay salaries based purely on DAUs or app downloads, but you sure can if you have enough revenue. Revenue can also allow you to avoid raising outside capital, or enable you to raise less capital at a better valuation, thereby retaining more ownership of your company.

Once you have the end goal in mind, you need to work backward. Let's use a fictional e-commerce company, Bob's Hats.

Potential investors want to see Bob's Hats hit $1 million per year in revenues. The first step is to develop a rough marketing model that shows how to get to $1 million a year.

In this case, let's assume the company has just launched and has some data from a handful of beta customers. (If the company wasn't live, they could go through the same exercise, but would have to make assumptions for all the data points we are going to review.)

Let's work backward and describe all the intermediate metrics Bob's Hats should be watching:

- The company has some early data that says that new customers on average place one order per year for $50. Hence, the company needs 20,000 customers to place an order in its first year to hit its revenue target of $1 million.
- The company has also seen that only 50% of the customers who put something into their cart actually check out. In other words, it needs to have 40,000 customers put something in the cart.
- Only 10% of the people who visit the site will put something in the cart. In other words, the company needs 400,000 people to visit the site in order to have 40,000 put something in the cart.

We now have a very rudimentary funnel. Acquiring customers is all about managing the funnel.

Sales Funnel

400,000 visitors

40,000 people put something in the cart

20,000 customers at $50 / order

Now that we have the funnel mapped out with goals for each step in the funnel, we can monitor progress to see if we are achieving our goals. If we are not achieving our goals, we can see where we are falling down and create strategies around those shortcomings.

Also, we can start to map out marketing activities that get us to the funnel numbers. In the case of Bob's Hats, we can figure out marketing activities that drive 400,000 people to the site. If we experiment with running ads on Google and discover that 1% of users who see the ads click on them, and that it costs $2 per click, we have learned two incredibly important things: First, if the company is going to rely solely on Google for new customers, it is going to cost $800,000 to hit the company goals. Second, the company needs to show the ads 40 million times to drive the 400,000 clicks, or visits, to the site.

Sales Funnel

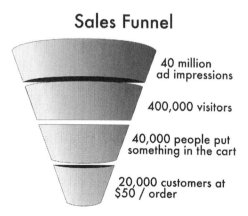

40 million ad impressions

400,000 visitors

40,000 people put something in the cart

20,000 customers at $50 / order

By the way, you might have noticed that we have extended the funnel to actions that happen outside of the Bob's Hats' site. The first step in the funnel is now showing an ad on Google 40 million times.

The company will likely want to experiment with a variety of vehicles like Google, social media, press releases, and more to drive users to the site, but that is getting ahead of ourselves. We'll get into a variety of different strategies a bit later in the book.

Is Your Speedometer Working?

Once you have figured out your funnel, it is time to figure out how to measure progress versus goals of each step. A great time to work on your measurement system is before the product launches. However, if your online business is already live, that is no problem — just get started now.

Dashboard for Key Metric

Below Target

Above Target

Most online businesses will use a web (or mobile) analytics tool like Google Analytics to measure customers flowing through the funnel. There are other analytics tools you can use, such as Adobe Analytics, but Google Analytics is the dominant web analytics tool in the market. Thus, we will use it here.

The most important place to start is by measuring your main objective (frequently referred to in online marketing circles as your "conversion action," in case you were looking for a new term to impress people at parties). In the case of Bob's Hats, the goal is $1 million in revenue, so they will want to measure revenue and, more specifically, orders, as their primary conversion action.

While you likely will get data on orders and revenues from your e-commerce platform, we would strongly suggest that you measure orders and revenue through a web/mobile analytics tool. We will talk about the advantages later, but the short version is that an analytics tool like Google Analytics will allow you to really slice and dice the data by various attributes (e.g., location, mobile device versus computer, etc.).

In Google Analytics, you have two different ways to measure major objectives like orders: e-commerce transactions and goals. We are big advocates of using Google Analytics' e-commerce tracking, even if you are not an e-commerce company. You want to track new paying users? Use e-commerce tracking. Just want to track trials? Use e-commerce tracking. And so on.

The beauty of e-commerce tracking in Google Analytics is that it shows up in most of the major reports in the tool. For example, if you look at a report of what countries your users are in, you will see how many actually placed orders in each country. The same goes if you are looking at a report to see how many users came from Facebook versus Twitter versus Google — you again will see how many orders were placed from customers coming from each of those places. In effect, e-commerce tracking constantly reminds you to optimize your site around orders and revenue. If we are trying to hit $1 million in revenue at Bob's Hats, we want our team very focused around orders and revenues.

The only real downside of the e-commerce tracking is that the setup is a little more involved than simply using goals. To set up e-commerce tracking, you will need to work with your web developers and/or designers. In most companies we have worked with, the setup is pretty trivial. However, we realize that technical capabilities can vary by team.

If you want a simpler approach, you can use goals in Google Analytics. The setup is often quite easy. You tell Google Analytics what page on your website (or event in your mobile app) represents success. For example, if you want to track orders, you tell Google Analytics what web address customers will hit when they have successfully completed an order. This is usually a "thank you for your order" type page. The setup is often easy enough that your average marketing person can do it in just a few minutes. (If you don't have a thank-you page with a unique URL, you will likely need to engage a designer with some technical skills.)

Google Analytics Goals

In Google Analytics, if you navigate to Admin → Goals and then create a new goal, you should see a place to enter a success page or event. Google even has a wizard to walk you through setting up the most common goals that people use. Once you tell Google Analytics that success page or event, you can use the verify tool to see how many goals would have been tracked over the past 7 days. If you are using a success page and you want to get fancy, you can tell Google Analytics that a user had to pass through one or more prerequisite pages before they got to the success page. This can help if people can get to your success page multiple ways, but you only want to track people who came through a certain path.

Goals do have the advantage that they have a very rudimentary way to measure upstream events in your funnel. In the case of Bob's Hats, you could measure how many people put something in the cart relative to how many placed an order. However, the funnel tracking in Google Analytics goals is pretty basic. If you use it, you will want to check your data using some of the techniques discussed later in the chapter.

The downside of goals in Google Analytics is that the basic setup we are talking about here does not provide very granular data, such as e-commerce tracking. E-commerce tracking gives you orders, transactions, SKUs purchased, and so on, all the way down to actual order numbers. With goals, you can track how many times they happened, but not a whole lot more. Also, the e-commerce data tends to be a little more reliable because you have actual order numbers, thereby allowing you to audit the data. With goals, you merely are measuring how many times a certain page is being hit, but there are times when customers refresh the page or hit the back button to go back to that page, thereby causing some erroneous data.

Whichever way you go, we would encourage you to get familiar with how Google Analytics integrates e-commerce transactions or goals into the basic reports. Go to the geography reports and see how many orders (or whatever your main goal is) you get from customers in various countries. Then go to the reports about what types of devices your customers are using, and again, look to see how many are placing orders from different types of devices.

Tracking your progress is like setting up the speedometer in your car: It is the main thing you will be looking at. However, you will need other measurements, so let's dig into the other steps in your funnel.

In the case of Bob's Hats, we said that we also wanted to track people who put things in their cart. One easy way to do this is to set up a goal (using the technique described above) for people who hit your cart page. The goal reports in Google Analytics will tell you how many sessions (i.e., customer visits) included a trip to the cart page. By comparing this number to the number of orders Bob's Hats gets, we can now see what percentage of users are putting something in the cart, but never checking out.

While the example we used for Bob's Hats just had a few major steps in our funnel, you can get very detailed. For example, you can track how many times people went to the cart, how many hit checkout page 1, how many hit checkout page 2, and so on. This will tell you exactly where people drop out of the process.

Sales Funnel

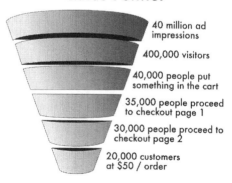

40 million ad impressions

400,000 visitors

40,000 people put something in the cart

35,000 people proceed to checkout page 1

30,000 people proceed to checkout page 2

20,000 customers at $50 / order

In the Bob's Hats example, we said that the top of the funnel was how many impressions we received and how many visits we got to the site. We can get visits from the standard Google Analytics audience overview report. Again, we can compare this number to the number of times people put something in the cart to see how many visit but never make it to the cart.

One key thing to remember is to use consistent units throughout your measurements to the furthest extent possible. Often sessions (i.e., customer visits) are the easiest units to use. You can also use unique users (although that typically takes a little more work in Google Analytics). The most important thing is to use the same units all the time. It is just like what your high school science teacher told you: Be consistent in unit measurement. If you can, stay away from pageviews. Users can hit pages over and over for a variety of reasons, and often it doesn't mean much. One caveat to these rules is that if you use the goal feature, it will report based on pageviews. So, that's another reason why we encourage you to use e-commerce tracking if you can.

Capitalize on What You Know Already

Before you go to the outside world to find more customers, it is important to understand as much as possible about any users you already have. Even if your business is just launching, you often have some beta users.

The first place to look is your "best" customers, where "best" can be those who keep coming back and using your site every day, those who are paying you, or those who are doing other valuable actions with your site. The first question to ask is, what are these "best" customers doing on your site or in your app? If you are an e-commerce site, you would want to look at what products people are buying most frequently. You would also want to see which products people are viewing most often.

If you are a site that is dependent on people coming back (e.g., an ad-based site), drill down to see what people are spending most of their time doing on the site. If you can, focus on those users who are coming to the site far more than other users. Is there some feature or content on your site that really hooks customers? The early employees of Facebook often talk about how they learned that once you had a certain number of friends on Facebook, you would be hooked. You are looking for something similar: What is your hook?

You will want to gather this data in three ways: through site or app statistics, surveys, and live discussions. Site or app statistics are often going to be your best bet because they give an unbiased view at what people are doing with your product. Companies most often are using Google Analytics or a similar tool to gather these stats. Use the data to see where your heavy users are spending their time on the site or app. Do you see any common themes that separate the top users from the more casual ones? To perform this analysis, build segments in Google Analytics. You can build a segment that looks only at users who hit a certain page, or users who spent a certain amount of time on your site (or have visited a certain number of times).

A second approach is running surveys. We recommend you keep the surveys really short and, ideally, build them into your product as much as possible. Try to have people answer 1, 2, or 3 questions right in the site or the app. Often it is effective to start with broad, open-ended questions like, "What do you enjoy most about our product?" You could be surprised that what the customers perceive to be your benefits are not exactly what you originally thought.

A final approach is to chat live with customers. At the end of the survey, you might have a checkbox asking if they would be willing to speak live with you. You then can follow up with a handful of those folks, offering them some small but valuable reward for their time (e.g., an Amazon gift card). If possible, record the conversation. You again will want to ask customers what they like (and don't like) about the product. What are the benefits? What are the features they use? How are they really using it? Although you won't mention these customers by name in your ads, you want to listen for words that come up consistently. Those are the words you want to use in your ads.

Next you will want to understand who your initial users are, particularly the top ones. A tool like Google Analytics can provide basic demographic data (i.e., gender and age). Alternately, you could capture some of that information in the sign-up flow. For example, a lot of sites ask your age in the sign-up flow to ensure they are not marketing the service to children. Let's say that your site attracts users of all ages, but your best users are 20 to 30 years old. That is very important information.

Site Demographics

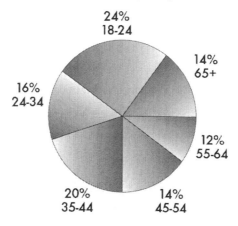

Similarly, it is often helpful to segment your users geographically. Are your best users mostly from one country, a couple states, or a few cities? If so, is there anything about those locations that is different than others? If you are doing well in San Francisco, Austin, and Seattle, it might mean that you are doing well with tech-savvy users.

You can use surveys and live conversations to fill in the gaps about your users. Are they from certain lines of work, or do they have common skillsets? Do they have common educational backgrounds? What else do they have in common? Sometimes the live conversations will unearth new theories that you would want to research further through surveys or analytical tools.

Once you have this information, you can decide what types of customers you want to go after in your first wave of marketing. If your best customers are currently 20- to 30-year-olds in Silicon Valley, you might decide to initially put more effort into attracting 20- to 30-year-olds in tech cities. Conversely, if you are seeing that almost no men over 50 are buying your product, make sure you are excluding from them your paid advertising to the extent possible. You are now building the parameters for your future targeted marketing efforts (targeted marketing refers to messaging specific types of people based on common characteristics). By refining who you target, you can dramatically increase your marketing efficiency. Often, it isn't a 10% to 20% increase in efficiency that you gain, but more like a 100% improvement. In the example above, you could spend a lot of money on men over 50, but if they aren't buyers, you are just lighting the money on fire.

While this strategy of targeting certain types of

people who are likely to be your best customers is highly effective, it has a major downside. You need to bear in mind that these audiences could be very different from what you will see when you go to a broader area. Marketing to a software engineer in Silicon Valley can be different than marketing to a farmer in the Midwest. Similarly, a software engineer is likely to use your product very differently than a farmer. If your end goal is to appeal to a broad audience, but you market the service to a much more narrow customer base, the feedback you get about your marketing efforts and your product might not help you in the long run. As long as you are aware of this limitation and realize that you are going after early adopters right now, you should be fine. Just start planning for how you are going to go after users who are not necessarily in the early adopter bucket.

Are You Ready?

One question we frequently get is, "When do I launch my customer acquisition efforts?" Usually what they are really asking is, "When should I start spending money on acquiring customers?" Unless you have some insanely popular product like Facebook, you will need to spend at least some money to jumpstart your launch.

This is a tough area with no clear answer that applies to all companies. If you wait too long, competitors can pass you by. If a competitor gets enough traction before you launch, it can be hard to catch up.

On the other hand, the risks to launching too soon can be even greater. If your user experience is poor, you likely will waste all the time and money you put into marketing the company. Worse, you might leave customers with a bad impression of the site and lose them forever, no matter how much you improve the user experience afterward. They might take to social media and tell others about the bad experiences they had. In fact, we guarantee this will happen if the experience is terrible. People love to be the first to tell their friends how terrible something is.

Here is a low-tech way of gauging whether you are ready to kick off your marketing efforts. Try to find a handful (say a dozen) people who are not familiar with your product but are good candidates for using your product. Ask them to walk through your sign-up flow and use your service exactly the way end customers would. Ask them for their feedback. Get the good and the bad news … especially the bad news.

A more formalized way to do the same thing is to contract with a user testing service (e.g., usertesting. com). You define what you want prospective customers to do and they will find users who match your criteria who can walk through your business and provide feedback. Typically, the users are recorded as they walk through your site or app. These sites usually are very cost-effective and can provide quick feedback.

After you have had some sample users walk through the site or app and you review the feedback and/or videos of the users, you should have a good feel for whether you are ready. Your site or app will never be perfect, but is it good enough that people will really enjoy it? If yes, then proceed.

ROAS: The Holy Grail—Spend Less than You Earn

A basic tenet of business is that while you need to invest to create your business, you cannot invest more than you plan to earn. Specifically, you cannot spend more on average to acquire each customer than you expect to make from that average customer over the long haul. Another way to say this is that your Return On Ad Spend (ROAS) — profits from customers acquired through advertising divided by the cost of that advertising — needs to be greater than 1.

Simply put, if you spend $1 on an ad to acquire a single customer, your hope is that the customer spends more than $1 on your site, or takes an action that your business values at over $1. If, for example, that customer places an order that generates $5 of gross profit (the amount you charged minus any costs of doing business), then your basic ROAS is 5:1, meaning your $1 investment returned $5. Of course, this is a very simple example, but it helps you understand the concept.

On the surface, this analysis sounds simple enough, but there are a lot of complexities. One of the first issues that comes up is what costs should you include. For example, should you include the cost of people or tools? Typically, we like to include costs that are variable — in other words, costs that will increase as you scale up your customer acquisition efforts. However, even that can be a little fuzzy. Maybe your team of three marketing professionals can scale advertising a lot, but at some point you need another person. Are people fixed costs that should be excluded from the equation, or are they variable costs that should be included? A lot of marketing professionals exclude headcount costs, but the important thing is to just be consistent.

Once you have decided what costs to include and exclude, you need to determine how many new customers your advertising brought in. For example, if you are looking at ROAS for paid search, you will want to look at a given time period (e.g., the month of August), to figure out total costs and the total number of new customers acquired. If you spent $100,000 and acquired 1,000 new customers, you spent $100 per new customer.

CAC and LTV

Simply put, Customer Acquisition Cost (CAC) is the amount you spend to acquire a customer. Advertising is part of the CAC, but there are often other costs associated with acquiring a customer.

Lifetime Value (LTV) is the value of the customer over their lifetime. The simplistic way to calculate LTV is to look at a set of customers, say those that signed up in August, and add up what you make from them. That means taking the gross amount they spend and subtracting out any costs. If you are an e-commerce site and you sell those customers $1,000 of goods per person, but those goods cost you $600 wholesale, you only count $400.

The trick of calculating lifetime value, especially for relatively new businesses, is that it is hard to tell how much customers will spend over time. This can get pretty tricky, so you might want to get your CFO or other financial person involved. However, the short answer is that you can *extrapolate. If your customers spent $100 this year, but one-third of the customers didn't come back the next year, you can assume a similar trend in your forecasting model. For newer companies, the figures are going to be pretty rough simply because you do not have a year's worth of data, but anything is better than nothing. The key is to be consistent across all your ad sources.*

One last tricky issue is that as a new company you are still trying to figure out what customers are going to spend. You are still playing with pricing, adding new products, and tweaking your conversion rates. Again, be consistent and remember when you are looking at your ROAS numbers, there is a fair bit of margin of error.

Now that you know how to calculate ROAS, you will want to start calculating it for all the acquisition sources we are going to talk about in the upcoming chapters. This will give you a feel for whether you are making or losing money on any given advertising channel. Don't be disappointed if you are spending more than you are bringing in initially — it takes a while to get things dialed in.

You also will want to drill down beyond just a given advertising channel. For example, instead of only looking at paid search, you will want to look at specific campaigns or keywords. More on that later. Above all else, use the data that you have, be consistent, and continue to measure as you collect more data.

Part II: Customer Acquisition Strategies

IN THE FIRST SECTION of the book, we talked about how to instrument your business to see what acquisition strategies are working, and which ones are not. In this section, we will transition to the main strategies for acquiring customers.

Bear in mind that many of these acquisition strategies are deep, complex areas that take years to master. These areas are changing quickly with prices and tactics that evolve day by day. Our goal is to give you an introduction to these approaches and cover the primary issues you will deal with as you get going, while at the same time, not overwhelm you with information.

While these strategies might seem like completely independent activities, we cannot overstate how much interaction there is between them. For example, if you run ads on Facebook or run pre-roll ads on YouTube, you are likely to see more people come through the search engines looking for your brand. We will cover this interdependence in several places later in the book.

Friends and Family

One of the best acquisition strategies to use early on is also the easiest: Leverage your networks. Start simple: How many people do you know? How many do you keep in touch with on social media? How many contacts do you have on LinkedIn? Now, repeat that for everyone on your team. It probably is a pretty significant number. Even more importantly, if you have been doing a good job of building your network over the years, there is a strong chance that most of those folks will have a pretty broad network as well (think 6 degrees of separation, or 6 degrees of Kevin Bacon if you prefer). This can be a very important springboard to leverage, especially in the early days of your online business.

There are a variety of techniques that people use to tap into their networks, but the key is to figure out what will appeal to the people you know. It certainly helps if you have an online business that appeals to a broad swath of the network(s) you intend to tap. Even if you don't, don't despair — you just need to tailor your message.

Typically, the most effective technique to use with personal networks is to offer them something really exclusive. Can you offer them access to a closed beta? In other words, can you offer them access to check out your business before it is available to the outside world? Done right, it can make people feel like they got exclusive access to something special — a virtual backstage pass. Companies will sometimes tightly control who accesses the beta and allow friends and family to invite a few people to use the service. This has the added benefit of encouraging your network to share it with other people. However, your offering needs to be really unique and new in order for this to work. HBO's *Silicon Valley* had an entire episode in Season 3 dedicated to this exact scenario.

Another approach is to give the product away for free for a limited time to people in your network. This works well for online subscription businesses and Software as a Service (SaaS) companies because they don't have a lot of direct costs per user, so there is little to lose. They give the product away to generate a buzz around the company and gather feedback, which is more valuable to the company than the cost of the giveaway.

If you are an e-commerce company, a related approach would be to sell products at your cost, or offer folks a really nice gift if they order in the early stages. Don't be stingy, especially early on. You need users to get the company going.

As you tap into your message, it is often helpful to ask for feedback on your business. Tell people you want them to write back to you (not a generic support email address) if they have any issues or have suggestions for how to improve the business. You might be surprised by how many people respond with very detailed suggestions. While you have to take every idea with a grain of salt, you might get some real gems from the feedback.

Also, you might be discouraged by some of the feedback you are getting. Try not to take it too personally.

We realize that sounds kind of ridiculous; how could you not take it personally? We know. Just do your best to look at the feedback objectively. Not every piece of feedback is relevant, so don't be afraid to dump the ideas that simply don't make sense. Look for trends, patterns, and other comments that make you say, "Oh … I hadn't thought of that."

You could also ask people if they want to be on your email distribution list to stay abreast of company updates. A lot of people like to stay in the know and will ask to be on the list if you are doing something interesting. By staying in touch with these people, you have the opportunity to remind them about what you are doing. They often will refer customers (or employees or partners) to you. The key is to find the right cadence. You don't want to bombard them with updates. You need to send them information when you hit a big milestone, launch some key new initiative, or have some other exciting news. If you are emailing these folks more than every two to three months, you probably are not being selective enough.

While friends and family rarely are enough to fully launch your online business, it can be a very powerful way to get started at next to no cost, while at the same time, collecting invaluable feedback.

Paid Search

When you go to www.google.com and type something in the search box, Google will show you a mix of paid ads and organic (i.e., free) listings. We will talk about organic/free search in a later chapter, but suffice to say that those listings are ones that Google shows because Google thinks they are the most relevant to what the person is searching for. The paid listings are ones that are shown based on Google's auction system. In this chapter, we will talk about how you bid on keywords in that auction system.

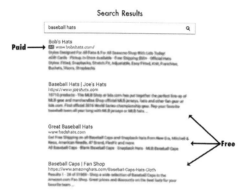

When it comes to paid search, Google has been the dominant platform for a while. For several years now they have had about two-thirds of the desktop market. Google's paid search platform is called AdWords. Bing is the other major player, typically with a little over 20% of the desktop search market. Bing's platform is called Bing Ads. As such, you probably will want to start with

Google and then move to Bing when you have a solid start on Google. We would also encourage you to keep a close eye on changes in this area. For example, paid ads in the Apple App Store are growing in importance.

Paid search is often one of the first customer acquisition techniques that companies use, for a variety of reasons. One of the main reasons is that it is easy to dip your toe in the water. You can set the budget to be whatever you want, and start testing.

Also, all things considered, it is relatively easy to get started with paid search. You don't have a lot of fancy ads to create. You are typically working with short text ads. Plus, you can start by bidding on a few keywords and see how it goes. You will learn a lot by taking a few different types of keywords and comparing the results of each against each other. You can quickly learn what types of ads work for your business, and which do not.

One of the other nice things about paid search is that it is often late in the buying cycle. You typically are dealing with customers who are searching for a given product, or type of product. While search doesn't work as well for new product categories, it can be very powerful if you play in a more established product category. You can acquire customers who are ready to buy at that moment or are close to making a decision. This allows you to acquire customers quickly and gain a lot of valuable data in a short time period.

If you are in a new product category, you might need to take a different paid search strategy. If no one is searching for your category of product (because they don't know it exists), one approach you can take is to bid on terms that are closely related to what you are doing. When photo books first came out, few people were searching for them. As such, online photo retailers had to bid on much more generic photo terms, and talk about photo books in the ads as a way to educate consumers. An alternate approach is to use some of the other channels described in this section, and revisit paid search later in your company's lifecycle.

So what keywords do you bid on? Luckily, there are a few easy ways to generate keywords that customers might be using to find you. A great starting point is just speaking with existing and potential customers to get their ideas for how they would use a search engine to find a product like yours. Second, there are a number of great tools for discovering keywords. For example, Google provides a powerful Keyword Discovery tool right within AdWords. SEMrush is also a great tool for investigating what keywords your competitors are bidding on.

Keyword Research

Keyword	Monthly Searches
baseball caps	40,500
baseball caps for men	4,400
black baseball cap	4,400
ball cap	6,600
baseball caps for women	5,400
black baseball cap	4,400

As you research keywords to bid on, it is important to remember that your customers might describe your products very differently than you do. If you have worked in the industry for a while, you probably have accumulated a fair bit of industry jargon. Customers most likely won't use those terms to find your products. They probably will use very simplistic terms instead. Also, they might use terms that are inaccurate. When we worked in the photo industry, we saw a lot of customers searching for things by the wrong name because they didn't know the proper name. Keep an open mind and don't exclude terms just because they are "wrong." The more customers don't know what to call your product, the more creative you will have to get.

Speaking of competitors, you might be tempted to bid on competitors' keywords or brand names. Depending on your competitive situation, that can be a really good source of customers. However, you can certainly get in a lot of hot water if you use trademarked terms in your ads, so you will want to avoid that.

One of the early topics that comes up is whether you should bid on your own brand name. For example, should Bob's Hats bid on the term "Bobs Hats"? The short answer is that you probably want to do some testing and see what works for your business.

On the surface, bidding for your own brand terms doesn't make a lot of sense. After all, if you search for your brand, you should come up in all the top organic spots, because Google will usually recognize your website as a strong, relevant result to a search for your brand (i.e., the Bob's Hats website should show up in the organic listings when someone searches "Bobs Hats").

However, there is a certain credibility in some customers' eyes that comes from seeing a paid ad in addition to seeing all the organic listings. As such, a lot of businesses find that running a paid ad on their own brand terms brings in more customers. Your site essentially shows up at least twice at the top of the page — once in the paid listings and at least once in the organic listings. You can run simple tests like turning brand ads off in certain regions or on certain days of the week. You then can measure conversions with and without the paid branded ads and decide for yourself whether it's worth spending marketing dollars on your own branded search terms.

One other thing to consider around bidding on your own brand terms is that by doing so, you can drive up the price for competitors who might be tempted to bid on your brand. While this might not be a big deal when you are first getting started, it is something to think about as you grow.

If you do run branded ads, you might want to think through who sees the ads. For example, if someone buys from Bob's Hats, we might not want to show them a paid branded ad when they come back a second time.

Be sure to keep a close eye on what searches the search engines match to your ads. When you are setting up your paid search program, you will tell the search platforms what types of keywords you want to bid on. Often, you will match for a lot of keywords that you never intended to match on. That is why it is important to run reports in the search platforms to see what actual customer searches were matched to your ads. You then can manually exclude certain phrases to really dial in which keywords you show for.

Be sure to investigate how you set up conversion actions in the paid search platform(s) that you use. In the case of Bob's Hats, we would want to tell AdWords and Bing Ads when someone places an order. This is relatively easy to set up and very powerful. When configured, you can see in very granular detail how much you are spending in AdWords and Bing Ads per order. Specifically, you will see the cost of a conversion (order or action taken) throughout AdWords and Bing Ads. For example, you can see the cost per order for a given campaign, a given keyword you are bidding on, etc. That allows you to quickly make changes to optimize your spend. Furthermore, the paid search platforms can automatically take action based on this data. For example, in AdWords you can set up multiple ads for a given keyword. AdWords then will start by showing the ads an equal percentage of the time. However, as AdWords learns which ads convert better, it will show more users the more effective ads. This is a great way to quickly learn what types of messages resonate with your customers.

When you are using paid search, create landing pages that are closely tied to the ads you are showing. If you have an ad for a given product, make sure that the landing page features that product as much as possible. The search engines will automatically review the content on your landing pages and how users interact with the landing pages to determine a quality score. Quality scores are a long and complex topic, but let's just say that they have a big impact on both what you pay for ads and where you rank on the page. Hence, you will definitely want to pay attention to these scores.

Do you go solo with paid search or do you get professional help in the form of a consultant or agency? Managing paid search can be very time consuming once you go beyond a handful of keywords. Plus, most professional consultants and agencies have powerful software that monitors AdWords and Bing Ads to automate the work. As such, while you might want to start your paid ad program yourself, there is a high likelihood that you will seek help once things get rolling.

SEO

Now that you know a bit about paid search, let's talk about its more outgoing and complex cousin, SEO (Search Engine Optimization, which we admit, does not sound very sexy). Let's say your paid search strategies worked well. Why not try to get some of those customers for free instead? That is essentially what SEO is all about: You are trying to show up in the search engine results most relevant to what the customer is searching for ... without paying to be there.

First, it is important to understand how search engines operate. When Sergey Brin and Larry Page were at Stanford, they laid out the plans for a new search engine called Google that would use PageRank as the basis for which sites were most relevant for a given search. Prior to Google, search engine results often were either 1) built by humans who compiled lists of the most relevant content, or 2) relied heavily on the content on the page. Using humans to build lists of the best content on the web clearly didn't scale. Could you imagine that job? There are nearly 650 million active websites, and counting!

Relying solely on the keywords on the page opened the search engines up to all kinds of manipulation by people who "stuffed" the same keyword onto a given page over and over, thereby tricking the searching engines. Sergey and Larry had a new approach that basically said that the most relevant results are ones that have the most links pointing to them, particularly links from high-quality sites. That is greatly oversimplifying things, but you get the idea. If you want more detail, you can actually read Sergey and Larry's paper online. Other search engines now more or less use the same general approach of evaluating how many inbound links you have to your content, particularly from high-quality sites.

As in the case of paid search, the place to get started is by understanding what keywords you want to go after. Luckily, you already built that list in your paid search efforts. You have a full list of all the keywords that you might be interested in, and you also know which keywords actually produce conversions. That is where you want to start.

Next, you need to think about what content you have that matches those keywords. While inbound links are important, everything starts with content. What typically works best is if you can give a list of keywords to whoever is writing your site. You will want to map one keyword (or a few very similar keywords) to a given page on your site. That means there is a good chance you will need to create more pages. SEO is like fishing. Every page on your site is like another line in the water. The more lines you have in the water, the more chances to catch fish!

A good writer will be able to update the content to work in the keywords without making them sound forced. You never want to give up the quality of your content just for SEO purposes. Your site can definitely sound like it was created by a robot if you focus too much on keywords and not enough on great content, and Google is sophisticated enough to recognize this and penalize you for it in search rankings. On the other hand, if you have a good set of keywords, you know the words customers are using to search for your product. That tells you a lot about how customers are thinking. Good content should be able to speak to customers in their own terms. Hence, SEO should help improve your content if it is done right.

Bear in mind that the search engines have to be able to find your content. It has to be "crawlable," to use industry jargon. If the content is hidden behind a password, is buried in an image, or requires you to load an app, the search engine likely won't be able to see it and include it in their results.

On each page on your site, there are ways to use HTML to tell the search engines more about your content, behind the scenes. This is a rapidly changing area, but we will describe three places that you definitely want to take a look at. Your web designer should know how to set up these tags in your HTML.

First, there is the title tag. The title tag is what shows up in the browser when you navigate to a given page. Think of it is as the very short description for that page. It is important for the title tag to incorporate the keyword you are focusing on for that page. When a lot of companies start up, they just put their brand name in the title tag on every page. That is basically giving the search engine just one keyword: your brand name. If you don't rank well for that already, and your site has been live for a while, you have a big problem! It is OK to include your brand in the title tag, but it shouldn't be the focus of the title tag.

Title Tag

Next, you will want to look at the meta description. Essentially, this is the description that comes back when searching Google for something. Remember that this is the information that users are seeing in the search engines when they are deciding whether to click through to your site. At a minimum, it will have a huge impact on whether users click the listing. That in turn is likely to impact your ranking. Write a short description that includes the keyword you are targeting, summarizes the content on the page, and entices people to click.

The last tag that you will want to think about is the H1 tag. On many web pages, you will see some big text at the top of the page that is essentially the main caption for the page. This main caption is often tagged with an H1 (in the backend HTML code) to indicate it is the main header for the page. That is sending the search engines a very powerful signal about what the page is about.

Now that you have the content on the page set up, you need to go back to the original premise of Google: You will rise in the search rankings if high-quality sites link to you. You can start by reaching out to other sites that you know and asking them to insert links on their site to yours. The more established the sites, the more value you will get. If you want to get fancy, you can use one of the tools that tries to measure the PageRank of a given page.

Moz, a powerful but affordable SEO tool, offers the ability to see what sites link to your competitors (or other sites in your industry). This is a great way to build a list of folks you should approach to see if they will link to you.

Ideally, you want these other sites to link to specific content on your site. In other words, for Bob's Hats, we don't want someone to just throw up a simple link on their site that says "Here is a link to Bob's Hats." That kind of link might help you rank for the keyword "Bob's Hats," but hopefully you are already doing well for that.

Instead, we might write articles on how to clean your hats, how to tell if a hat fits, or a hat style guide. Creating that type of content has a multitude of benefits. First, other sites will be much more inclined to link to you. If other sites find the content is helpful to their audience, you might not even need to ask.

Second, you now have multiple pages, other than your home page, that are showing well in search. This gives you more lines in the water to catch fish. These pages are going to rank for keywords that go way beyond your brand name.

Lastly, if these articles are well-received by consumers, they are the types of things that consumers are likely to click on from a search engine, and even share on social media.

This all comes back to creating fun and engaging content on your site. A lot of people create content on their site simply because they feel like they have to. That content on your site is only going to help if your audience really digs it. If the customers really like it, the content is likely to help your SEO efforts in a lot of ways.

It is important to build a process for ensuring that your site has good search engine hygiene. For example, if you have broken links on your site, search engines won't be able to crawl your site and might penalize you for having bad links. If you convince others to link to you, but you then move the pages, thereby breaking the links, you will be undermining all your hard work. If you have multiple pages with the same title tag, you are again undermining your SEO efforts with duplicate content, which Google recognizes and penalizes you for.

To keep your site clean, we particularly like the Google Search Console and Moz. The Google Search Console is a free tool that Google provides to webmasters. It can provide you with a very basic audit of your site. We mentioned Moz earlier; one of their core features is a powerful site audit tool. Note that these audit tools are not perfect — they just give you a starting point for looking for trouble.

If you have started to deploy some of these tactics, you have probably noticed that SEO can be very time consuming. Creating great content takes a lot of work! However, some sites have customer-generated content. Public discussion groups are a great example. Customers are talking about various topics, thereby creating new content all the time. As long as search engines can reach the content (i.e., no password is required) and the content has good SEO hygiene, you can derive a lot of benefit from this customer-generated content.

Bear in mind that a lot of sites have cases where some of the content on the page is created by the company, and some is created by consumers. A great example is e-commerce sites that allow for consumer reviews. The product description comes from the company, but the reviews are customer-generated. This means that new content is being created all the time, something that will help you with search engines.

If you have a site with a fair bit of customer-generated content, you should be dedicating a decent chunk of your time to SEO. Depending on what kind of content your customers are creating, you might be able to drive a lot of your customer acquisition strategy with this customer content.

It goes almost without saying that customer-generated content can get out of hand. It definitely opens the door to everything from scammers to hate-speech issues. You need to think through whether you will review what content is posted, and if so, how that process will scale.

Another related topic on SEO strategy is User Experience (UX). To borrow a term from Forbes, SEO can easily stand for "search *experience* optimization" these days. The primary point is to create a good experience on your site. Do not have pages or features that do not work properly. Pages should load quickly, your site should be visual with simple navigation, and people should easily be able to do what you want them to (or what they intend to do) on your site. For example, if you sell products, then the shopping and purchasing experience should be as close to flawless as you can get it. Google measures time on page and it is important to SEO as well: The more time on your site people spend, the more they are consuming your content and/or products. Google will reward you for this. Create a good experience, and your SEO efforts will show it.

We'll add one more point to the SEO discussion, and it's a big one: mobile friendly sites. Google and other search engines have placed major emphasis on rewarding sites that are mobile friendly and punishing those that are not. This relates back to the user experience point above, in that Google wants to send visitors to sites that will give them a good experience. A site that is not optimized for mobile traffic (people visiting on mobile phones or tablets) can create a frustrating experience on a small-screen device. As such, Google made major updates in 2016 that push mobile friendly sites higher in search results. The two options to meet this criteria are to design a mobile version of your site, or design your site using a responsive platform. A responsive website, as the name suggests, is a site that "responds" to the device that the user is on. It is smart enough to detect if you're on your phone or your desktop, and the display changes to best fit the device. This is our recommendation, as most website design platforms are now responsive, whether you use a do-it-yourself platform like WordPress or hire a designer.

One key thing to remember about SEO is that it is a long-run strategy. It is very rare that you do something and suddenly have a huge SEO spike. It can happen, but it is the exception and not the rule. On the other hand, if you build high-quality content that ranks well on a given topic, you often will see results from it for years to come.

SEO is a complex and fast-changing area. We just gave you the basics here — we didn't want your eyes to gloss over from technical details. If you start to see some traction, consider hiring a part-time SEO consultant who can help you dive deeper.

Social Media

Given how many people social media platforms reach (nearly 2 billion worldwide in 2017), and how much time people spend on the platforms (100 minutes a day on average in 2017), social media can be a great way to attract new customers. However, there are a lot of facets to social media, and many are not well understood.

First, it is important to figure out which social media platforms are a good fit for you. Facebook, Twitter, Pinterest, Instagram, Snapchat, etc., all appeal to different types of users. It is impossible to cover all the social media platforms, especially since new ones seem to be popping up all the time. You want to think about how many of your potential users are on each platform.

With over a billion users, Facebook is pretty hard for most companies to ignore. Having said that, it is worth doing a little simple market research of potential customers and/or existing customers to see which social networks they use.

Next, it is important to understand that, much like search, there is an organic side of social media, and a paid version. Often, the two sides are highly intertwined, also like search.

On Facebook, you can set up a page (or multiple pages) for your company and start posting content for free. Similarly, you can create a Twitter handle and start reaching out to your followers. However, these tactics are unlikely to bring you many new customers for free.

Unless you pay to advertise, your followers are likely to be existing customers, for the most part. In other words, you're likely interacting mostly with your existing customer base. This interaction is great for collecting feedback and informing your customers about new features and new products, but it doesn't get you new customers per se.

In addition, using Facebook to interact with people who have liked your company's page no longer works particularly well, unless you spend some money. Facebook has, over time, reduced the number of people who see your company posts, unless you pay. Several studies have said that as few as 3% of the people who liked your company page will see a given post, unless you pay to boost your post (it is usually pretty affordable to boost your posts to increase the odds that your followers see the content). Now you are into the world of advertising on social media!

There is one case where social media can bring you new customers, without spending to target new customers: by producing viral content. If you create super content that your users want to share, you have the ability to get a lot of visibility on social media for free. Let's say you create some content that is really funny or really insightful and post it on Facebook, and tweet it out, and so on. If your existing followers really enjoy the content, they might like and/or reshare the content with their followers. If their followers also enjoy the content, the cycle can continue for quite a while. We will talk about this strategy, often described as content marketing, in a later chapter. However, let's just say for now that producing really compelling content is not easy.

In addition, there are a lot of ways to advertise on social networks. One of the easiest ways is to take the content you are already posting and just broaden the reach. For example, on Facebook, you can boost your post to reach people who liked your page, and their friends as well. In a lot of cases, the friends of your existing customers can be excellent targets for your product, because they share the same interests as your customers.

On Twitter, you can employ a related tactic: Show your content to all the followers of a given handle. For example, you can show your content to all the followers of a key company in your space. Alternately, you can show your content to all the followers of a competitor.

Most of the social networks also allow you to advertise to potential users based on interests, demographics, location, and the type of device they are using. These can be fairly broad brush tools and your success with them will largely depend on two things. First, it will depend on how closely the interests overlap with the type of customer you are looking for. Second, your success will often depend on your ability to layer many of these criteria on top of each other. While the interests might be a bit broad for you, you could find that your conversion rates rise dramatically as you focus on certain regions, certain demographics, and certain device types.

A word of caution is in order at this point. While Facebook often states that you can advertise on their platform with a minimal budget, the reality is more complicated. With paid search, you can see results immediately, but when advertising on social media, have patience. In social media advertising, you will constantly be testing different ads with different types of targeting, so it can take a while to get the economics dialed in.

For example, Bob's Hats could target anyone who likes fashion and reach a large audience. But, if the marketing gurus at Bob's Hats use its existing data to further target a more specific audience (such as people who like trucker hats that live in southern California and use iPhones), the company will likely increase its conversion rate.

One of the most interesting options available on social media is the ability to upload an existing customer list and advertise to customers who look like your existing customers (aka look-alike lists). Many of the social networks have a tremendous amount of knowledge about their users. When you upload your existing customer list, they will find the commonalities between these customers, and then find other users with similar traits. This type of advertising can be particularly cost-effective. Note that each social media platform has its own algorithm for building look-alike audiences. Some of these algorithms are better than others, and the success rate varies by type of product. Because Facebook has such a vast audience and knows so much about its users, it is a natural place to start with look-alike audiences.

From this perspective, it becomes clear that Facebook and other social media platforms are essentially huge databases masked behind a fun, human-connection interface. People readily and willingly share information about themselves that advertising agencies would have loved to have had back in the day — and we all do this freely! Every time you like a page, you are telling Facebook more about you (and in some cases, about everyone in your network). If you pay to play, you can tap into this information and target exactly who you want based on the information that is collected every time a person posts, shares, likes, and comments on a social network.

This is just a taste of the targeting capabilities that the social media platforms offer. Bear in mind that social media platforms are changing constantly, frequently adding new targeting options. They also tweak the existing options and the names of the functionality. Given that social media is a very rich environment to acquire customers, you will need to invest a significant amount of time to keep up-to-date with the latest best practices (or hire someone who can do this for you).

Video

Video has become a target-rich customer acquisition medium. As of this writing, YouTube reported that they have a billion active users each month, and that every day, users watch hundreds of millions of hours of video. Furthermore, Facebook is making a big play in video and there are plenty of other video networks out there. As a society, we sure do love our videos, especially those that involve cats!

Not only does video provide a large audience, but the format lends itself better to certain products. If you have a new product, or one that is a little more complex, it is hard to describe it in a short text ad on search, a static banner ad, or even a still photograph. However, with a 15-second video, you have the opportunity to tell your story. Similarly, if you have a product that has an emotional appeal, you'll have far more success on video than search. Let's say you were introducing a new sports car. Search ads probably wouldn't do it justice. However, a fast-paced video with a mix of great product shots, roaring engine sounds, short sequences of the car tearing up country roads, and dramatic music is likely to make people want to buy the car. It just has a different appeal.

YouTube is the obvious place to start with video because of its vast reach. Like search, YouTube has two sides: organic (i.e., free) and paid. If you upload a video and use keywords and a description optimized for SEO, you might be amazed by how many views you get.

You can help your chances for success by doing keyword research the way you did on search. At the same time, sometimes it comes down to a little luck. You might upload a video today, and years later, the video could become popular and get hundreds of thousands of views due to some public event. We have personally been involved in a number of those situations. The more videos you have, the more chances you have to get lucky. Remember to really focus on SEO tactics.

A great example of this is how some power tool companies make how-to videos that feature their products. People might search "how to install a cabinet door," and if the company's video is optimized properly, the video will show up. The user then can use the video to learn home repair skills, and the company can market their tools and hardware to the user.

You will likely want to set up a company channel on YouTube so users can view all your videos. If they subscribe to your channel, they will be notified of new content, thereby guaranteeing that new videos get a certain level of exposure. This also allows you to create playlists and autoplay the next video for people interested in your content.

In addition to the free side of YouTube, you can pay to get in front of customers. YouTube offers a variety of ad formats, but the pre-roll format is the one most people are familiar with. Your video will play before the user gets to watch their content, similar to a commercial on TV. Depending on what options you select, users might or might not be able to skip past the ad after a few seconds. YouTube offers extensive reporting on how much of your videos customers watched.

Video Pre-roll Ad

There are a variety of options for specifying which customers you want to reach, ranging from keywords to interests to customers who have visited parts of your site (aka retargeting). Having said that, many advertisers find that it takes some time to really dial in their targeting. YouTube's audience is so vast that if you set your targeting too broadly, your ads will be shown to lots of people who are not in your target market, thereby driving down cost effectiveness.

One great way to ensure that you are reaching your ideal market is to target people who view videos on a given YouTube channel. You can scour YouTube for channels that are a great fit for your customer base and tell YouTube that you just want to advertise on those channels. Since some channels don't allow ads, you might not get a ton of reach, but you are guaranteed to be reaching a very focused audience that hopefully is a really good fit for your business.

Reach

Reach typically refers to how many people in a specific marketing vehicle could see your ad. It does not mean how many people will actually see your ad — that depends on your budget and bids. Reach is about the hypothetical maximum number of people who could see your ad.

One of the keys to succeeding on any video platform is creating great content. While video is very time consuming (and expensive) to produce, there are many more options for producing content these days, and the tools are far more available. A simple animated video can be relatively affordable to produce, something that wasn't the case 10 years ago.

Your content strategy will vary a lot depending on whether you are focusing on organic or paid traffic. If you are going the organic route, you will generally want content that is educational, emotional, and fun to watch. If users really enjoy your content, they will share the content through social media and subscribe to your channel.

If you are paying to show your video on YouTube, you can create content that is a little more ad-oriented. It is still a good idea to create something fun and engaging so people will watch the videos and share them, but you can tell them more about your product than you would with a video that was focused on organic traffic.

As part of launching your content on YouTube, you will want to think through what your call to action is for a given video. You might want people to subscribe to your channel, visit your site, or view another video. You then can create cards in YouTube that encourage people to take your desired action.

It is important to keep in mind the context for how users will see your paid ads on video. When users are on search, they often have intent to buy a product in your space. They are very far down the sales funnel. When they see the ad, they generally will click if the ad looks appealing.

With YouTube, you often are reaching people who never thought about buying your product, or never even knew it existed. This is the top of the funnel. Even more importantly, people are on YouTube to watch the video they were looking for, not your ad. Even if they watch your video through to completion, they are trying to get to *their* video. That means that you might not get a lot of people clicking through and then ordering your product on your site. Regardless, YouTube is highly important. It is reaching new customers and often giving them a very good picture of what your product does.

YouTube provides reporting on how many view-through conversions you are getting. View-through conversions are when someone watches your video, doesn't directly click on the video to go to your site, but does return to your site within some specified (and often short) time period, and completes your conversion action. For example, someone watches your video, and then the next day, looks you up on search, comes to the site and makes a purchase. For this reason, YouTube and search often are highly interlinked. Although it is hard to completely attribute these conversions to

YouTube, YouTube played a part. Attribution tracking will be discussed more in the chapter titled, "Don't Get Too Focused on the Last Click — A Word on Attribution Tracking."

If you have good luck with YouTube, you might want to try video on Facebook. Facebook is putting an increasing emphasis on video, and the options are expanding all the time. Plus, given Facebook's enormous reach, it is a video platform that you cannot ignore if video works for you.

While YouTube and Facebook have a massive reach, a variety of other video platforms exist. These range from video ad networks to small sites that stream custom content. While the range of choices can provide you some interesting options to reach your audience at very affordable prices, we would encourage you to fully optimize YouTube and Facebook before you move beyond them, especially if you are considering doing advertising on specific sites. Your time is one of the most valuable commodities, and YouTube and Facebook offer you the ability to reach almost every Internet user on the planet.

Partnerships

One of the most overlooked customer acquisition strategies for the early days of a company is partnerships. The basic concept is to find other companies that are targeting the same audience, but are not competitive. You then approach those companies and find a way to work together. For example, Bob's Hats could partner with a hunting site to sell hunting hats to their customers, and the two companies would work together on joint promotions.

There is no magic bullet for finding potential partners. Usually, it requires spending a fair bit of time searching on Google for companies in your broader space. If a company shows up for a lot of searches, they might be someone you want to talk to.

Similarly, you might want to look on YouTube to see who shows up in your space. Who comes up for common searches? Do their videos appeal to your customer base?

You might already have an idea of organizations that fit this mold, especially if you've been in your industry for a while. Tap your network and recall those conversations had on the trade show floor or at industry events.

Building a list of potential partners from scratch can be quite time-consuming, so this is a perfect area to consider hiring an intern. Often, interns will be quite efficient at scouring the Internet.

Once you find potential partners, the question turns

to what kind of deal you might strike with them. If you are tight on funds, you might want to strike a cross-marketing deal where no dollars are exchanged but each company promotes the other. The other option is to pay the partner to advertise for you. Since most companies don't have a set pricelist (aka rate card) for promoting other companies, the prices can be all over the board. Some advertising can be incredibly affordable, and some can be ridiculously expensive.

If you want to strike a cross-marketing deal, the first thing to understand is their relative size compared to yours. There are a number of tools (e.g., Alexa and Mattermark) that track how many website visits and/or mobile downloads a company gets. On Google Play, you can see how many times their app has been downloaded. On social media, you can see how many followers they have.

If the company is about your size, you might have a decent shot at doing some cross-marketing with them. Perhaps they mention you on social media, and you mention them. Similarly, you could mention them in your newsletter or link to some of their content to help their SEO in exchange for a similar treatment from them. You just need to get creative. Sometimes some cool schwag and a few introductions will be repaid with some nice recognition by the other company. As long as you have similar customer bases and you don't compete, there will be a lot of options to make something work.

Approaching a company that is a lot larger than yours about a cross-marketing deal can be tricky in a couple ways. First, the other company might be inundated with partnership requests. As such, it can be difficult to break through the clutter. Even if you do break through, it might be tough to offer them something that is appealing to them. An email swap or other cross-marketing deal can be tricky if you have much less to offer. That isn't to say these deals cannot be struck, but it is really important to understand the objectives of the company you are approaching. Sometimes the company will have a unique goal that they are trying to address that you can help with. Examples could be an introduction to someone they are struggling to meet (who you might by chance know), or advice in a certain area. Larger companies might also be attracted to the PR perspective of partnering with a small start-up. Creativity is definitely the name of the game.

Influencer Marketing

Sometimes you find people in your space who have the ability to reach out to (and often influence) hundreds of thousands, or even millions of people. These are people who have built up significant audiences, and these audiences trust the influencers tremendously. If you can work with them to help get the word out about your company, you can gain an incredible number of new customers, often at limited to no cost. Bob's Hats, for example, could tap a fashion influencer to post several pictures of the influencer wearing various Bob's Hats products.

Fashion Influencer Promoting
Bob's Hats

Influencer marketing is very similar to partnerships, and often the line can become blurry between them. We typically think of partners as companies or organizations with multiple people, whereas influencers are often just one person with a lot of influence in your space. Regardless of where you delineate things between influencers and partners, the techniques you will use for both of them are very similar.

In fact, when you are searching for partners, you are likely to stumble upon individual influencers. While search engines are often an effective way to find partners (because they have fairly established web presences), you want to rely more on social media tools to find individual influencers. Many influencers have a large presence on one or more social media platforms, but don't put as much emphasis on their web presence. Thus, a tool like Hootsuite or Radian 6 can be helpful for finding influencers who are active on social media in your space and have a large number of followers.

It goes without saying that there are a lot of social platforms, and to be really thorough, you need to search across a number of them (either directly or through a social media tool). We have seen cases where the most important influencer in a given space was on a social media platform that was not necessarily top of mind. For example, we know of influencers who have hundreds of thousands to millions of followers on Google+, a platform that many of us don't always think of as a popular social media platform.

Similarly, many influencers have big presences on

YouTube (they even have their own title: YouTubers). As such, it can be worth spending some time searching YouTube for channels in your space that have a larger audiences.

Once you identify potential influencers, you can often start by liking and resharing their content. They will always appreciate that, and might do the same for your content.

The next logical step is to reach out to them and determine if there is a way for you to work more closely together. Some influencers are willing to create promoted posts for small amounts of money. Others are more interested in early access to cool products or even free products. You just have to listen to them and see what is appealing. Since many of them are individuals, money talks, even in relatively small amounts.

Bear in mind that most influencers need to create educational and informative content for their audiences. If you can help them do that, they will be interested in working with you. However, that does not mean just pushing out a marketing piece or ad for you. They often will be more interested in doing a review of your product or a content piece about your space. Review the content they are publishing, listen to what their goals are, and try to propose things that are consistent with their goals and that their audience will enjoy.

Press Relations (PR)—Getting the Attention of the Media

"Alas, if I could just get an article in the *New York Times* or the *Wall Street Journal* (or substitute in the name of some other high-profile publication), I would be all set! I would have all the customers I need to launch my new business." Sound familiar? Many online businesses have had this thought at one point or another. However, press relations (i.e., getting the attention of the media), rarely plays out this way.

First, let's step back and remember that journalists are there to write newsworthy content. Announcing that your company has launched, or that you have a new product or feature, might not be newsworthy in their eyes. Journalists are deluged with press releases from companies making all kinds of announcements. In reality, many of these announcements are not interesting to the journalists you are trying to attract. These journalists see so many announcements that it takes something pretty unique to catch their attention. It doesn't mean you shouldn't try, but you do have to be realistic about what is likely to be picked up and by what type of publication.

There are a lot of ways to cut through the clutter of press releases that hit your average reporter every day, and almost all of them revolve around creating an interesting story that doesn't sound like a marketing brochure. For example, one approach is to do some interesting market research about your industry. Run a survey on a major online platform, and collect data from hundreds or thousands of people. Ask them interesting questions that could make for an interesting story. For example, if you are in the online security business, perhaps you could ask people whether they have been the victim of identity theft or a similar crime, or ask how concerned they are about being a victim of identity theft. If a lot of people say they have been a victim, or are worried about being a victim, that could be the basis of an interesting story. This kind of story might only mention you as the author of the survey, but it will cast you as a thought leader in the space.

Another approach is to take an interesting customer and write about their experiences. Perhaps you have a customer who is serving a good cause or has a fascinating story. Write a press release about that customer (assuming you have their permission) in a way that is interesting, and would hold the attention of the average writer.

As you get larger, another approach you can take is to talk about significant milestones you have crossed. Try to pick unique metrics — lots of companies talk about how they hit X customers. By contrast, look at how YouTube often talks about how many hours of video their users have consumed. That is a fascinating metric and one that very few companies can talk about.

Even if you cannot write a press release that really catches the attention of reporters, you should still issue press releases, for a few reasons.

First, it can be hard to predict which press releases gain attention. Sometimes you will be pleasantly surprised when a relatively mundane release catches the attention of a reporter.

Second, if you host the press release on your site, you would be amazed by the organic search traffic that some press releases get. The results vary a lot from industry to industry, but in some industries, press releases mesh well with the types of keywords that potential customers are searching for.

Next, let's turn our attention to what types of

publications you might want to go after. After all, you cannot just issue a press release and expect everyone to pick it up and start writing about you. You or a PR firm needs to pitch the media story ideas. That means having a hit list of folks to reach out to, and then aggressively contacting them.

While everyone dreams of getting an article in the big publications like the *New York Times* or the *Wall Street Journal*, be careful about what you wish for. First, those publications pride themselves on rigorous investigative reporting, meaning that they are likely to really probe your product looking for weak spots. If they find issues or think that competitors are superior to you, they will write about that. If you are a young company, that type of press can really sink your ship, not only with consumers, but also with potential investors and business partners. You want to make sure your product is really ready before you go to the big guys.

This goes without saying, but getting through to the largest publications and the hottest writers is very difficult. You can spend a lot of time trying to get them interested without ever attracting their attention.

Even if you get an article with a national publication, the results might not be what you expect. Often, a big article will bring a lot of awareness to your company, but it doesn't mean that you will get a zillion orders that day or that downloads of your app will go off the charts. These national articles are great air cover, but you still need to be doing a lot of the other acquisition techniques we cover in this book. A national article works well if it is accompanied by, say, a huge push on Facebook, lots of ads on YouTube, and widespread local radio advertising. People need to hear your company's name a few times before they take action. Also, consider tying in a promotion of some type to help get the conversion over the goal line. People might hear about you in various marketing channels, seek you out, and if you appeal to them with a promotional offer, the chances of conversion are much higher.

At the other end of the spectrum are your local newspapers. They often are looking for good news about local companies that are just getting off the ground or are hitting interesting milestones. As well, they tend to go a lot easier on the companies they are writing about, so your odds of getting a positive story are much higher.

Another route is to approach industry publications. Are there publications that focus on your industry? While they have a smaller readership than, say, the *New York Times*, they might hit a broad swath of the key buyers in your industry. As in the case of the local newspapers, they often are a little hungrier for good content and tend to be a little easier on the companies they write about.

As you think about which media organizations you want to approach, there are two common mistakes that people make. First, they underestimate the impact of social media. Many news outlets have a limited number of print or online readers but have a robust social media following. If they write about you and mention the story via social media, the article can travel the globe for days via social channels. Sometimes it is the smaller publications that have the energetic social media audiences that are more likely to share the article, thereby extending the length of time the article is seen.

A second thing that people overlook is the value of SEO. Some publications are highly visible on organic search. We have seen numerous cases where an article on a relatively small site drives traffic for 5 to 10 years after the article is published. If the site does a good job in the SEO realm, their articles can show up for years to come. If, over time, you build up enough of these articles, it can really build your traffic. Plus, these types of articles often are highly credible to potential buyers.

Another PR approach we have seen work well is approaching industry groups. Some industries have an email list or social media presence that hits all the movers and shakers in the industry. In these cases, get to know the people behind the newsletters. That means going to the industry tradeshows and meeting the people who organize the industry group. Sometimes buying someone a meal or a drink goes a long way toward a nice mention in an upcoming newsletter to the industry. Use LinkedIn for this strategy as well. Join industry groups on LinkedIn to grow your network without spending a dime.

Along the same lines, many industries have analysts who track the industry and put out reports on companies in the industry. Similar to the industry groups, it is best to get to know these analysts at a more casual level. Proactively reach out to them and try to meet them at major tradeshows, especially when you are not pitching any new news. You want to get to know them and let them know you are available if you can be of assistance to them. If they call you for information, be helpful and provide them as much information as you can (without giving away any secrets of course).

Affiliate Marketing

Affiliate marketing is one of those avenues that sounds great on the surface but can be difficult to execute, and definitely doesn't fit all businesses. Affiliate marketing essentially means that you find affiliates — companies or individuals — who will market your product for a success fee if the customers they send your way complete some conversion event. For example, you might pay out $X per order or Y% of order revenues they send your way. Alternately, you can pay based on new trials or new customer accounts created. The attractive piece, from a risk perspective, is that if they are not successful, you don't pay them. Sounds great, right? But it isn't as easy as it seems.

First, let's talk about how affiliate marketing works. There are several major networks that essentially act as clearinghouses between companies that are looking for affiliates to market their products, and affiliates who are willing to pitch products in exchange for a success fee. The largest of these networks is Commission Junction. Other networks include Share a Sale and AWIN (previously Affiliate Window). When you go through the network, you make a deposit with the network. They keep track of how much you owe the affiliates and ensure the affiliates get paid appropriately. Bear in mind that you do get to approve each transaction before the affiliate is paid.

So, how can you lose? Here are some of the complications. First, if you are a relatively new company, you might have a tough time attracting affiliates. The networks sometimes suggest that if you just join their network, affiliates will flock to you. However, it typically takes work to reach out and recruit affiliates to work with you. Sometimes you have to entice them with upfront payments to get their attention.

Secondly, there are some categories of products that work better with affiliates than others. Affiliates are generally pretty used to working with e-commerce sites, particularly certain categories like fashion and electronics. If you have a really new product or service, affiliates might be unwilling to take a chance with you.

The challenge with affiliate marketing is finding high-quality affiliates. Because you pay based on a success basis, the industry can attract some shady players. For example, you will see affiliates that place fake orders and later reverse them. If you are auditing the orders carefully, you can easily catch the egregious cheaters.

However, there are more subtle cases to watch for. One trick that affiliates will sometimes use is to bid on your brand keywords to draw in traffic that already knows about you. Often these affiliates will only bid on your brand outside of your home state so you won't easily see their ads. To catch these sort of cheaters you can use a brand identity tool like BrandVerity, or hire a consultant or affiliate manager who uses such a tool. (More on consultants and affiliate managers in a bit.)

There are a number of other approaches that affiliates can take to try to take credit for customers you already acquired and educated about your product. Consumers can install toolbars that give them some sort of points or dollars off on certain purchases. These toolbars essentially will intercept customers who were already coming to your site and take credit for them. In other words, you are doing the marketing work, but the affiliate is taking credit.

One of the best ways to catch folks who might be doing shady stuff is to audit the affiliate orders by affiliate, looking at what percentage of new customers the affiliate sent you. If they sent you all repeat customers, there is a high probability they are intercepting your existing customers by doing something fishy.

Another option to stay out of trouble is to work with a consultant or affiliate management firm who knows the players in the space, and who can steer you toward quality affiliates. Because of some of the issues mentioned above, the industry is very tight; most of the reputable players have known each other for years. Along these lines, there are several affiliate marketing events each year (e.g., CJU), where key players in the industry come together. It is a great place to vet a lot of affiliates in a short time by asking basic questions about how the affiliates work. Plus, the really shady affiliates generally don't show up in these in-person events.

Customer Referral Programs—Getting Your Customers to Spread the Word

If you can make it work, one of the most cost-efficient customer acquisition programs is a customer referral program. Here's how it works: You get your customers to refer new customers to you, sometimes in exchange for some small reward. That's it.

This is every company's dream. The challenge is in making it work. Let's face it, most people are pretty selective about referring their friends and family. Who wants their friends and family to be spammed by some company they don't know or aren't interested in? Therein lies the reason that most referral programs fail.

Many marketers offer customers a reward for referring friends. While it sounds good on the surface, the reality is that for some customers, it makes the whole proposition that much more sleazy. As a matter of fact, many companies find that they get more referrals when they offer no reward, or a reward that is not monetary (e.g., access to a special feature if they refer friends).

Along these lines, one of the approaches that works well for some companies is to spin the customer referral program in a different light. They tell the customers, "Share this with a friend who could benefit from this product (or content)." The key is to make the pitch be very benefit-oriented. For example, if you save people money, ask them if they know anyone who should be saving money through your product. This different spin can have a big difference in how people perceive things.

If you can integrate referrals into your product, then you really have something special ... which is the perfect transition into the next chapter: virality.

Virality—The Age of the Cat Video

We've all done it. You go online and see the most outrageous, or funny, or heartwarming, or poignant video (or other piece of content), and you send it to your friends, family, or colleagues. How cool would it be if that content somehow drove people back to your site or promoted your company in some way? Virality is essentially that — you create something so compelling that people have to share it. If done well, your message/brand/product gets shared at the same time.

Virality at Work

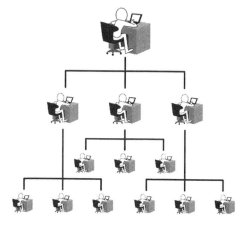

When we worked in the photo industry, virality played a very important role in customer acquisition for the popular photo printing sites (e.g., Shutterfly, Snapfish, etc.). These sites allowed users to upload photos and share them with users. Often, these photos were very widely shared: vacations, pictures of the kids, shared memories with your inner circle, and so on. The recipients of these shared photos would then share the photos with other people. At a minimum, all this sharing resulted in a lot of brand awareness for these companies. Better yet, the recipients of these shared albums uploaded their own photos, thereby continuing the virality effect by sharing photos with a whole new set of people. The best outcome? Some recipients created accounts, uploaded photos, shared them, and placed orders for prints and photo products … all because another user shared content.

Although it would be great if your site had the virality of the latest cat video, the reality is that virality is equally difficult and important. You don't need to swing for the fences. Lots of little base hits will go a long way, because virality is free, and if it is done right, it just keeps repeating. Plus, the bigger you get, the more referrals you get.

When we talk about virality, there are a couple metrics that you need to understand. The first is how many people a user shares with. In the photo example above, when someone uploads a photo album and shares it, how many people do those photos get shared with (either directly or indirectly)?

The second metric to understand is what percentage of those recipients become users. If 100 people are invited to view the shared photos, what percentage actually create their own accounts?

If you want to get fancy, you can compute a viral coefficient. The viral coefficient, known by industry insiders as K, is the number of people who the site/content is shared with, multiplied by the percentage of those people who join your site. If your viral coefficient is greater than 1, you have a self-sustaining viral product. In other words, you are well on your way to having the virality of a cat video. Congratulations! However, even if your K is lower than 1, it doesn't mean you are doomed. Remember, all virality is essentially free marketing, so take whatever you can get!

The final metric in virality is the most important: virality cycle time. The virality cycle time is how long it takes from when a user shares content or a site with others to when those downstream users turn around and start to share the content or site with others. In the photo example, how long does it take from the time a user shares photos to the time when the recipients have created their own accounts, uploaded their photos, and shared them with new people?

Virality cycle time is key because it has an exponential effect on your virality. Cat videos are wildly viral because the cycle time is super short. Someone shares a video with you and says it is super funny. You watch it almost immediately and then decide to share it with others, sometimes before you even finish watching it. The virality cycle time can be mere seconds, which is ideal for this strategy.

Now that you understand virality and how to analyze it, what do you do? The first thing is to measure your virality (assuming you have some part of your business that is viral). Dissect the three metrics we talked about above and think about how you are doing. If your users don't share with many people, can you encourage them by making the share functionality more prominent? Can you encourage more sharing by giving people lots of ways to share (via email, via Facebook, via Twitter, etc.)?

If people are sharing a lot, but the recipients are not coming back to the site and creating their own accounts, you need to think through how you are doing the sharing. Maybe your emails or your social shares are not compelling. Maybe you should give people an incentive to set up their own accounts. Many of the photo sites gave users free prints if they set up a new account after they viewed shared photos. The photo sites could afford to be generous given that this was essentially free customer acquisition.

If your cycle time seems slow, you can sometimes create incentives to encourage people to move faster. In the photo printing example, the sites could have encouraged more photo sharing by offering additional benefits to users who quickly shared. For example, upon joining, they could offer more free prints or a discount to users who shared photos within a certain timeframe. Obviously, you have to be careful about people gaming the system (e.g., creating lots of accounts just to get the free prints), but given that you are acquiring customers for free through virality, you can accept a little fraud that sneaks by.

If you don't have any virality today, start by sitting down and brainstorming simple virality experiments. "Share this with a friend" buttons might not get a ton of traction, but they can get you started. As you get familiar with virality and start to measure it and optimize it, you can bite off bigger experiments that are more integrated into the core functionality of your site or app.

Podcasts

Podcasts have exploded over the past couple of years, providing you with a wide variety of audiences and shows to choose from. This presents several advertising opportunities. First, some shows might have a great overlap with your potential customer base. This is particularly helpful if you have a fairly narrow customer base you are going after. You might be able to find podcasts that target your customer base in a way that few other vehicles can.

In addition, if you find a podcast that is a particularly good fit for your customer base, the hosts might be willing to integrate it into the show. They could mention that they have used the product, or casually drop references to your product, thereby providing you with a tremendous product placement.

Having said this, podcasts come with a number of limitations. First, the most common metric around podcasts is downloads. However, just because someone downloads a podcast doesn't mean they heard your ad or even listened to the podcast.

Second, because people are often multitasking while listening to a podcast, they might not remember your ad. Obviously, the better the ad and the better the fit with the listener base, the more likely you are to be remembered. Still, it isn't easy to cut through.

Even if the listeners do remember your ad, they might not be in a position to purchase your product right then and there. They might be in the car, out running, or out hiking. By the time they get back to their computer, they might have forgotten about purchasing your product. Hence, podcasts can often be better for building brand awareness than driving immediate sales.

Another challenge around podcasts is tracking actual purchases. Because users aren't clicking through on a digital ad, it is much harder to track conversions. The most common way to resolve this is to offer a promo code if your site supports this, then measure the orders or conversions placed using that specific promo code. Alternately, you could set up a vanity URL for customers. For example, mention the URL OfferXYZ.BobsHats.com or www.BobsHats.com/OfferXYZ in your ads, where OfferXYZ is whatever special offer you are going to give listeners. Yes, you should give them an offer to incent them to order later, since many won't be in a position to order at that time. Between your promotion engine and your web analytics tool, you hopefully will be able to track people coming to these custom URLs.

Podcasts are something you will want to test and see how they work for your business. At the same time, understand that without a full brand awareness study, it probably will be difficult to gauge the full value of podcasts.

Offline—Yeah, It Can Still Work

Offline advertising for an online business? You bet — it can work! With so many traditional advertisers moving online, there can be some real bargains in offline advertising. Having said that, there are some challenges, so it probably won't be the first place you turn.

The challenges with offline marketing largely mirror what we described for podcasts. Tracking is problematic, and often you will hit customers when they are not in a position to make a purchase at that moment. The tracking techniques we described for podcasts (e.g., promo codes and vanity URLs) can be applied to all these offline marketing techniques as well.

If you had success in podcasts, a natural extension is radio. Again, you will want to look for shows with a very direct overlap with your target customer base. In addition, you will want to push for shows that can go beyond playing your spots, and instead integrate your product into their shows. Radio is nice in that the cost of producing ads can be very reasonable. In fact, in many cases, the show hosts will just read your ads over the air, so all you have to do is provide the text.

Another vehicle worth testing is print. You can often find very specific publications that focus on your audience. Many of these businesses might be struggling financially, due to consumer media trends preferring digital to print, so you often can drive a hard bargain and get extra exposure. That can mean extra impressions on their online site or a feature in an article as well; media companies will often bundle print ad packages with an online component.

Tradeshows and conferences are one of the tried-and-true vehicles that work well in some industries. If there are a handful of shows where a large percentage of your customer base gathers, tradeshows are probably for you. If Bob's Hats specialized in superhero-themed designs, Comic Con is probably worth attending. Alternately, are there shows where highly influential people in your market, including members of the press, go to learn about the latest products? If so, again, tradeshows could be interesting.

There are some real pros and cons about tradeshows. On the positive side, you get to talk to potential and existing customers face-to-face. That is a great way to learn more about their needs, how they perceive your product, and how they perceive your competitors. You can also interact directly with your competitors, either out in the open or incognito, to see how they are positioning their product.

Furthermore, in a tradeshow environment, you sometimes can spend more time describing your product to customers. You can go beyond the sound bite and really define what you are doing.

The major downside of tradeshows is that they can be very time consuming for your staff, and the costs can quickly escalate. You have to be there before the show to set up, and be there after the show to tear down and ship things back to the office. For a typical show, you might be gone 3, 4, or 5 days. Think how much you can get done in that time.

Costs can really accumulate as well, because tradeshows charge an arm and a leg for things. It isn't uncommon to see shows try to charge several thousand dollars for decent (at best) Internet connectivity in your booth, or $500 per hour for required union labor to install your equipment.

Beyond the costs, tradeshows can be really hectic places where it can be tough to grab the attention of attendees. Look for ways to cut through the clutter. Sponsor a key talk, have a unique booth, or offer attendees some sort of relaxing or exciting break off the tradeshow floor that they cannot resist. Get creative! Years ago we attended a tradeshow in Orlando in the middle of the summer. It was brutally hot. One of the vendors took the initiative to order some margarita machines and hosted an impromptu margarita party by the pool. They probably bent a few rules with their party, but everyone at the show remembered them! The important thing is to get creative — don't be like everyone else, and don't assume that the action has to happen only on the tradeshow floor.

TV is another offline marketing vehicle that some companies will want to consider. Obviously, the investment is much more significant. It requires a fair bit of time and money to produce quality ads, and buying time for the ads to air can also break the bank. Super

Bowl, anyone? If you have had good luck with video on YouTube and other online video networks, TV might be for you.

Also, get multiple uses out of your TV ad content. We mentioned Super Bowl ads … the trend over the past few years for companies has been to leak the Super Bowl ad on YouTube a few days before the game. This generates buzz for the ad, and also helps reach those people that don't watch the game, or miss the commercials because the guacamole bowl is almost empty, or fast forward through the commercials. It also gets you more bang for your buck by not putting all your eggs in one basket, or in this case, by not spending all your money on 30 seconds in the second quarter. This same concept applies to companies that don't have the budget for a Super Bowl ad: Put your TV commercial on YouTube, on your website, on social media, and so on to get more value out of it.

The interesting thing about TV is that it is moving into the category of online marketing. Many TVs are connected TVs, and more people are bridging the gap between how they use their connected devices and their living room TVs. Consumers are signing into accounts, downloading apps, and connecting media to their home TVs. They are also viewing online content through their TVs (e.g., Netflix and Hulu). As this pattern continues, TV ad networks can leverage the digital data similarly to how online ad networks serve banner ads on websites. For example, rather than buying a commercial for a specific show, you might soon be able to buy TV ad space based on who's watching the show. Also, don't be surprised if you start to see more banner and pop-up ads on TV shows. Pandora and Spotify allow you to listen to music for free, but also force you to listen to ads from time to time, unless you pay to be ad-free. We might soon view TV advertising as an online marketing channel, rather than an offline one.

Content Marketing

One of the major themes in this book is that great content is essential. A lot of people talk about content marketing as an acquisition vehicle. However, that is a bit misleading. Great content doesn't attract new customers by itself. Great content is the grease that makes the entire online marketing machine move. It attracts visits via SEO, it makes your social marketing strategy go viral, it makes people read your email newsletters, etc.

A lot of times, companies create the content they want their audience to read or consume, instead of creating the content their audience really wants. This is a flawed strategy — you are only going to get great results by creating content that is compelling to your audience.

In order to appeal to your users, you need to really understand your target customer. What are your customer segments? For each of those segments, you will want to interview them, perhaps by phone or in person, to really understand their perspective. Ideally, you will understand the following:

- What are their pain points? If your content can explain how to solve a pain point, people will listen. Remember the power tool video example?
- How much do they understand about your product and space overall? Are there certain concepts that they are confused about? For example, are people confused about why they need a certain feature, or do they have misperceptions about what a

certain feature will do? Alternately, are there common myths that buyers in your space hold? If you can debunk myths or clear up things that people are confused about, you can again gain the attention of your audience.

- What are the phases of their buying cycle? If this is an impulse purchase, you might not have phases. However, if it is a complex product, you might have multiple steps in your buying cycle. For example, first customers might want to know if you can solve their issue. Next, they might want to know how you are different from others in the space. After that, they might want to understand the technical implementation required, followed by the support options available.

From there you can branch into online research. For example, you can look at keyword search volumes. What are the most common questions people are asking on Google? You can also look at sites like BuzzSumo that show what content people are sharing.

At this point, you want to take each customer segment and think about the content they would be interested in at various stages of their engagement with your company:

- Top of the funnel. These are visitors who might be generally interested in your space, or are just learning about your company for the first time. To appeal to them, you often will want educational articles about your space. Perhaps you can explain topics people are confused about. There is a good chance that the articles won't mention your company or your products specifically. You are just trying to set your company up as a thought leader in the space.

- Middle of the funnel. These are people you have in your database but who haven't started the buying process. For these customers, you want to offer them content that starts to educate them about the types of issues that your product addresses. Again, make the content educational and don't push your products specifically. The content shouldn't be like a marketing brochure. Make sure you are answering questions that your audience is actually curious about.

- Bottom of the funnel. These are prospects actively engaged in evaluating your product. Now you can start to more specifically mention your product in the content. For these visitors, you will want to understand the various steps in your buying cycle and what moves prospects from one stage to the next. For example, if customers at a given stage are trying to figure out the technical implementation process for your product, focus your content around answering that one question.

Remember that visitors at each of these stages need different content for each customer segment. That can wind up being a lot of content.

Your goals for your content will vary a lot depending on where you are using it. If you are using content for top of the funnel SEO purposes, your goal might be to drive as much organic search traffic as you can to your content. If you are creating content for a newsletter (middle of the funnel), you might be looking at how many people read the article, or how many share the content. If the content is bottom of the funnel content sent via a drip email program, you might measure it by how many people progress from one stage of your sales funnel to the next.

Part III: Maximizing Your Traffic (Squeeze as Much Juice as You Can)

IN THE SECOND PART of the book, we talked about various ways to drive customers to your site or app. Now we turn our attention to maximizing what you get out of that traffic. How do you get more juice out of the same number of oranges?

Most online businesses convert only a tiny percentage of the people that come to their site or check out their app. A 2% to 3% conversion rate is typical for turning visitors to buyers for many e-commerce businesses. Other business models, be it SaaS, paid content, or gaming, have similarly low conversion rates. They are paying all this money to get customers to check them out, but 98% leave without paying them anything. If they were physical stores and 98% of the customers came in only to browse, something would be seriously wrong. In the online world, low conversion rates are a fact of life for many companies. But luckily, there are a lot of things you can do to drive conversion rates up.

Moving your conversion rate from 2% to 3% at first blush feels like a small change, but it can have profound implications. In many cases, it can mean the difference between a positive or negative return on ad spend. That in turn means the difference between a scalable business … or one with no future.

Now that you are starting to drive traffic from various marketing campaigns, one of the things you will want to pay close attention to is the shape of your funnel. More specifically, how far do visitors make it through your flow? Let's say you have five steps in your flow. You will want to calculate the percentage of people who go from step 1 to 2, step 2 to 3, and so on.

As you calculate the percentage of visitors who drop off at each step, you will want to look for places where you see large numbers of customers dropping off. Most funnels have big drop-offs in one or two places. That is where you will want to focus your efforts using the techniques in the next couple chapters.

On a related note, we will also cover techniques for getting customers to come back to your site to take another look at what you offer. Most of these techniques are far cheaper than trying to get totally new customers to come look at your product.

Let's face it — many products are not impulse purchases. The more complex and expensive your product, the more you likely will need to stay in front of customers, encouraging them to learn a little more about you so they will think of you when they are ready to make a purchase. Would you ever buy a car after seeing just one ad? Probably not, but an ad can draw you in, and follow-up marketing campaigns can keep you engaged until that day when you are ready to buy the car.

AB Testing Makes Everything Better

AB testing is one of our favorite customer acquisition tools, if not our very favorite. We know what you're thinking: nerd alert! But seriously, this stuff is critical to your success ... and very cool.

AB testing involves showing some visitors who come to your site (or app) one thing, and showing other visitors something else. You then measure the results to see which variation had more success driving whatever goal you are focused on. For example, perhaps you test two different variations of your home page with different messaging to see which one drives more orders.

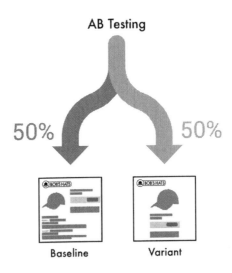

You can actually test more than two variants at a time, although the more variants you test, the longer the test will take. You will almost always have your current site be one of the variants you include in the test. That is your baseline. If another variant beats the baseline, then after the test, you should update the site to the variant.

Technically, AB testing isn't a customer acquisition vehicle, but it should be one of the core tools in your toolbox. When you AB test, you are optimizing your funnel, often improving the economics for every customer acquisition channel we talked about in the earlier chapters. In a lot of cases, you will find big gains in your conversion rates, especially early on. It isn't unusual to hear about companies that increased their conversion rates between 30% and 100% (on a relative basis) because of AB testing.

Doubling your conversion rate can have profound implications. Let's say you have a lot of keywords in AdWords that are slightly unprofitable. If you double your conversion rate, those keywords are probably all profitable. That means you have far more keywords that you can leverage, greatly expanding your profitable reach. Even better, if it is an increase in your general conversion rates, it impacts all of your marketing channels, from video, to paid, to social, to word of mouth. Said another way, a doubling of your conversion rate is like your boss walking in and announcing that your marketing budget has been doubled. How often does that happen?

What should you test? The short answer: everything! You want to get in the general mindset that you are always testing A versus B versus C, even if it isn't a true AB test. Do you have a lot of banner ads that you need created? AB test one contract designer versus another. AB testing can be applied to all aspects of your business.

The most obvious place to start is by testing your ads. AdWords is a great place to start because it has a robust AB test platform built in. You can try different creative and see which has the best cost per conversion. Google will even automatically send more traffic to your best performing ads.

Many other channels don't offer true AB platforms, but if you are careful and you show multiple ads to the same audience during the same time period, including the same days of the week, you often can get a good comparison.

Your home page is the next logical place to AB test. You probably get more traffic on that page than any other page on your site. As such, you will get results faster on your home page, and the results will be more meaningful.

If you use landing pages that are tailored to some of the acquisition vehicles described earlier, they would be the next obvious place to AB test. Remember, you should be using landing pages that are tightly connected to what you are advertising. If you are advertising a specific product or feature, drive people to the page that best describes what was in the ad — or create a page for the ad. These landing pages often get a lot of traffic, and you often are spending a significant amount time and money to send people to these pages.

When you think about what to test, it is best to start with bold variations. There is a tendency to test lots of small tweaks. For example, if I change the button from blue to red, does that drive more orders? Think bigger, especially when you start. Perhaps test your current design with one that is completely different. Test lots of text against lots of images or a video or two. Test providing customers with fewer products to choose from, or fewer menu choices. Try changing the order flow up, removing, or tweaking the steps.

When a bold variant tests well, it usually has a very big payoff and has implications for how your whole site is structured. By comparison, testing font size and button color usually has a very small benefit and has few implications for the rest of your site. Save the font and color experiments for when you are further down the road.

If you want to run an AB test on your site, you will want to use an AB testing platform. Optimizely is one of the better known products in the space. You insert a snippet of their code on your site and then use a visual editor to create variations of pages in your site. Your average marketing person with limited design skills can even run some basic tests using the editor.

For more advanced tests, you will need to engage a web designer or developer. Be sure to configure the goal tracking to measure the key goals for your site (as we talked about earlier). Most of the time, it doesn't matter whether more people clicked on a given button — you want conversions. As such, measure your variations on whether they drive more conversions.

The good AB testing platforms will handle all the math for you and tell you when you have enough data points to stop the experiment. Don't stop the experiment early; it is easy to get excited about the early results and call the experiment off too soon. That will lead to faulty results. Keep running the test until the platform says it is over. The only exception is that if the two variations are a draw, you might have to manually conclude the test.

If you are running an AB test outside of an AB test platform (e.g., comparing two competing ads on some advertising platform that doesn't have an AB test engine), you can do the math yourself. A simple Z test will serve most purposes. You can search online for web pages that handle the calculations for a simple Z test for you.

> ### Z Test
>
> A "Z test" is a statistical test that tells you whether one population (e.g., a group of users who saw variant A of your ad) is different from another population (e.g., the users that saw variant B of your ad). You provide the conversion rates for each group of users and how many users are in each group. The Z test then tells you whether there is a statistical difference between the two groups. This is important because you might see a difference in conversion rates across groups, but the difference is not large enough to be statistically significant. Therefore, you won't be able to conclude that one variant is better than the other one.

The main challenge of AB testing is getting enough volume to draw statistically significant results. In the early days especially, you needed to let an AB test run for months to get to a conclusion. That means you should test the really big changes first. Worry about little tweaks, like color and font changes, later.

To pick the best tests early on, be sure to consult a user experience expert if at all possible. Experts in this area can usually draw up a solid list of things to test that could produce big results.

Another challenge around AB testing is that it requires patience. No one likes waiting weeks or months for tests to conclude, especially when they are convinced their variant is right. Gain agreement from folks right up front that you are going to let experiments run to conclusion, and set expectations, even if it requires them to exert enormous patience to do so.

Even if a test fails, it is never really a failure. Think about that for a second. We have run hundreds of unsuccessful tests that we thought for sure would be winners. However, it is really hard to predict human behavior, so we are regularly surprised. Every customer base and every online business is different, so expect to be surprised. When a test fails (i.e., the variant you test actually drives down the conversion rate), learn from it. What did it tell you about how customers think? How can you apply that lesson to do the opposite of what you just tested? The bigger the failure, the more you often learn. Keep an open mind, and never assume anything.

Micro Tweaks—Going Deeper

Let's say that as you start to measure the effectiveness of your marketing channels, you notice that your customers keep dropping off in large numbers at a certain stage in your funnel. For example, customers start the checkout process, but an unusually high percentage drop off of a given page. You have highlighted the issue through web analytics, but you don't know exactly what to change.

As we have talked about, you AB test alternate versions of the page against the current page to see if they make a difference. However, if you don't have a good feel for what the issue is, you might be shooting in the dark.

There are a couple types of tools you might want to employ to deduce what is going on with the page in question. Heat map tools like Crazy Egg are a good place to start. You can hook up these tools with some simple tracking code and almost immediately start tracking where on the page users click.

Often you will find that there is something about the page that is causing people to click in the wrong place. Maybe your users think an image is clickable when it isn't. Alternately, maybe a lot of people are clicking on a button that you didn't expect a lot of people to click on. Is the text confusing, or are people just confused about what the next step is?

If your page has a form that users have to fill out, perhaps there is something confusing or broken with that form? To figure out what is going on with your form, you can use a form analytics tool like MouseStats. These types of tools can provide very granular detail about how far customers are making it through your forms. For example, they tell you how many people made it through a certain field, how many characters they entered, and how long they spent on that field. They also can provide playback capabilities to watch users going through your forms.

Every site is different, but there are a couple places you might want to start with these tools. First, you might want to see if there a certain field where a lot of users bail. Do customers make it through the first couple fields, but rarely fill out the 7th field? If so, that field might be confusing, or it might be a sign that the page is just too long.

Similarly, if you notice that customers are lingering on a given field that should be really straightforward, you might want to consider whether that field is confusing. This is especially true if a low percentage of users complete that step.

If these tools narrow down your problem, but you still are confused about what your issue is exactly, you might want to use user testing, a concept we discussed earlier in the book. This will give you commentary from live users, allowing you to really understand what people are thinking.

Email Marketing

When online marketers think of how to stay engaged with a lead, they often think of email. In this chapter we will cover newsletters, drip email programs for leads, and triggered emails.

One of the easiest email techniques to use is a newsletter. On your main landing pages, you might want to have a call to action that encourages customers to join your newsletter distribution.

Email Newsletter

We all get too much email, so you need to offer a hook to encourage people to cough up their email address. For many businesses, the two most common ways to get people to join the newsletter are special offers and engaging content.

Who doesn't like getting a deal? As consumers, we can be tempted to join a newsletter to receive special offers. If your site has a lot of special pricing offers, this might be a good fit. This is especially true if your product is one that has a shorter sales cycle and/or requires less investigation. If users join your newsletter and get special offers, might they be tempted to make a purchase?

Good email marketers build up information about what their newsletter recipients are interested in, and tailor the offers to those interests. If you sell clothing, and the person who joins your newsletter is a male college student, you shouldn't send him offers for women's apparel (unless your data tells you he is a repeat customer who buys women's clothing for his girlfriend or mom … but we are getting ahead of ourselves). If the offers are a mismatch for someone's interests, they will unsubscribe quickly.

As you get more sophisticated about your email program, you can layer in the recipients' behaviors. You can observe what emails they open but don't click on, what they do click on, or what they have purchased in the past to really tailor the offers they see.

Having said all this, there are a number of downsides around basing your newsletter program on promotions. First, as mentioned above, promotions work better for products with shorter sales cycles where customers simply need a little extra nudge. Second, promotion-heavy newsletters might not be a fit for your brand. If you have a premium brand, it might be incongruous with discounting.

The other major tact you can take with your newsletter is to create engaging content for your newsletter. This keeps you in front of the customers and reminds them of your company. The great part about this strategy is that can work for a wide range of products, and often is especially effective with more complex products with longer sales cycles.

The biggest challenge with this type of newsletter strategy is that creating great content is hard. Good writers can be tough to find, and even more importantly, it is demanding to keep producing content that customers want. Lastly, you have to be patient and realize that you might have a tough time linking a given newsletter to purchases.

Creating content that customers want to read is the key to this strategy. Unfortunately, most companies start with a different angle. They ask the question, "What can I write that will cause customers to favor my product?" That strategy is seriously flawed. Customers will quickly tire of articles that are basically thinly veiled marketing pitches.

The best way to start the content creation process is to sit down with real customers and ask them what challenges they have. What would they like to learn more about? What topics are they confused about?

From there you can branch into online research. For example, you can look at keyword search volumes. What are the most common questions people are asking on Google that pertain to your industry or product? You can also look at sites like BuzzSumo for this insight.

The great thing about this kind of content is that it can also be used in your SEO efforts via landing pages on your website, so it does double duty for you.

Just remember to not settle for so-so content. This entire strategy relies on customers loving your content. If they love your content, they will read more pieces on your site, and will have a positive image of your company when they are ready to buy. If you try to turn your newsletters into "marketing" articles, you can do more harm than good.

While we have focused so far on newsletters, they are not the only type of email to consider. Another common email program is called a drip email program. In this case, you send follow-up emails to prospects via a lead nurturing program like Pardot or Marketo.

The idea behind these drip programs is to move people through the sales cycle the we way we discussed in the content chapter earlier. In other words, you want to segment your prospects, perhaps by role or product that they are interested in. You then want to automatically send them content that is consistent with where they are in the sales cycle. Make sure it is appropriate for their role.

For example, if you believe that someone is in the technical evaluation stage and they are a technical person, you want to send them automated emails that help them with their technical evaluation. You still want to provide information that is educational, but the whole goal is to give people enough information to be able to move on to the next stage of your sales cycle. In the case of Bob's Hats, your emails to merchants and retailers that buy hats by the hundreds are a lot different than your emails to consumers looking to buy only one hat. Going deeper, your emails to that same audience will vary based on where they are in the buying process.

Drip email programs are successful when they help move more people through the sales cycle. If you can push more people from an initial lead status to a qualified lead, or a qualified lead to closed-won deal, your drip program is working. As we have talked about throughout this book, a good initial measure of your success in this area is that people are reading your content. They will only do that if the content is engaging and highly readable.

Drip email programs typically refer to emails that are sent to prospects. This same type of technique can be applied to visitors once they become a customer. These are often referred to as "triggered emails" because they are triggered by the user's actions in the system.

One example is a welcome email series that is triggered when a customer joins. In this case, the timing is based around when the customer joined. In other words, the customer might receive the first email X days after they join, the second one on day Y, etc.

Welcome emails often are geared around introducing

users to your company. Again, you will want to survey users to understand what kind of content is most helpful. You can interview people who joined your site a while back and ask them what kind of information was most interesting or enticing to them at that stage. Was it a video on how to get started, an email listing the support options, or a set of frequently asked questions (FAQs)?

There are many other types of triggered emails that you can use to bring users deeper into your site or encourage them to buy more. For example, if you run an e-commerce site, you might consider a special offer after an initial purchase to encourage customers to make a second purchase. Alternately, you might consider a "win-back" email after someone has gone dormant for a certain amount of time, or an offer to complete a purchase after a customer has placed an item in the cart, but not made the purchase after X days.

In the end, all email marketing is about sending customers the information they need, not the content you want them to see. Do that, and your email program will blossom with time.

Retargeting / Remarketing

Another marketing technique that can bring customers back to your site is retargeting (aka remarketing). The basic concept is that you tag customers who come to your site but don't convert, and then show them ads as they travel the Internet. Again, you've seen this before — you check out a pair of shoes on Amazon, don't buy them, and then head over to Facebook, only to see an ad for the exact same pair of shoes.

Retargeting

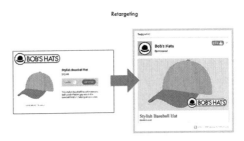

Because you are only showing ads to people who took the time to visit your site (or some subset of your site), you are advertising to a much smaller audience than you are going after when you are trying to convince people to visit you for the first time.

One of the benefits of targeting such a focused audience is that often, visitors to your site will come to the conclusion that you are much larger than you really are. They will say things like, "You must be doing really well — I see your ads everywhere!" Little do they know that you are not running ads everywhere — you just are chasing them around the web.

The first thing to think through is what you are trying to accomplish. If you have an e-commerce site and someone perused some product pages or even put the product in their cart, maybe you want to give them a reminder nudge a bit later. Perhaps the person was checking the product out while they were on the subway home but was not in a position to make a purchase. However, it might be that a later reminder can convince them to actually pull the trigger.

Alternately, if you have a product that requires time to investigate and consider, you might want to have follow-up ads that encourage people to learn more about your products, your company, or the product category in general.

Once you have determined what your goals are, it is time to think about how to segment your visitors. Some examples of segments you might want to consider include:

- Visitors based on what products or product categories they viewed
- Visitors that put something in their cart but never converted
- Recent customers

Once you have created your segments, consider what kind of messaging you want to use for each segment, and what the timing might be. If you are just trying to nudge someone who put something in their cart to complete the purchase, your messaging might be fairly straightforward. You might be able to get by with an image of the product in the cart, or an offer (such as a small discount) if they come back and buy. You probably want to remind people fairly quickly, and if they don't convert within a certain time period, you can simply shut off the ads.

On the other hand, if you are trying to move customers down the purchase path on a complex sales cycle, you probably want to create a variety of messages over a certain time period. For example, you might go with message one for the first X days, and then message two for the next Y days, etc.

Another thing to consider is frequency — how often your ads are shown. If you have a long sales cycle, you might want to pace your ads over time. If you have something more time sensitive (such as a seasonal product), you might want to be more aggressive about showing more ads in a short time period.

Finally, you will want to test different types of retargeting ads. For example, you can use basic banner ads, Facebook ads in users' newsfeeds, or video ads on YouTube. Once again, consider your message and pick the format that fits best with that. For example, if you have a complex product and are trying to push users down the sales funnel, or you have a product that has real emotional appeal, video might be a great option.

Part IV: Operating the Machine

MUCH OF WHAT WE discussed thus far paints the picture of you being "the man or woman behind the curtain." Let's spend a few moments discussing how to keep you customer acquisition strategies — your machine, if you will — well-oiled and operating smoothly.

There Is No Silver Bullet

The most common line of questions we get is, "What's the best customer acquisition channel for me to use? Should I use Facebook or search or [fill in the blank]?" These questions really miss the most critical point of customer acquisition. Customer acquisition is about having excellent tracking and analytics so you can see what is working. We like to joke that your approach should be to try a bunch of stuff and see what sticks to the wall. Perhaps a more professional way of saying it is that you should come up with some hypotheses about what works, try them, measure the results, and then evaluate what you want to do next.

Customer Acquisition Data

	Source / Medium	Device Category	Transactions
1.	autoemails / email	mobile	142 (1.24%)
2.	autoemails / email	desktop	939 (8.23%)
3.	(direct) / (none)	desktop	2,731 (23.93%)
4.	google / organic	desktop	2,387 (20.92%)
5.	(direct) / (none)	mobile	313 (2.74%)
6.	google / organic	mobile	273 (2.39%)
7.	autoemails / email	tablet	22 (0.19%)
8.	member_invitation / email	mobile	22 (0.19%)
9.	google / cpc	desktop	1,108 (9.71%)
10.	(direct) / (none)	tablet	76 (0.67%)

Let's get more specific about how this works. If you are using Google Analytics, one of your main reports will be the Acquisition report by Source and Medium. If you set this up properly, you can see how many sessions and conversions you gained by each site that is sending you traffic. You can see how many sessions and conversions you gained from free search vs. paid search vs. Facebook vs. YouTube. This report also does the math to show you a conversion rate for your visits.

Furthermore, you can add secondary dimensions to this report. For example, you can look at conversions from Facebook by the type of device the customer was using. How many Facebook customers were on a smartphone versus a tablet versus a computer? Alternately, how many came from one country versus another? You can also drill down to which ads you showed (assuming you tagged the ad with a tracking URL that included the specific ad that was shown). You can then cut the data a ton of different ways in Google Analytics and most web analytics programs — you just need to figure out what the most important ways are to segment your customers.

From here, you will want to take things a step further and figure out the return on investment on each of your channels. To do that, you will need the cost for each source you are tracking. Google Analytics does allow you to import cost data and then compare that to revenue it's tracking. However, a lot of folks might want to take a different approach, at least to start. You can export the data from the Acquisition by Source and Medium report into Excel. Even better, if you are comfortable with Google Sheets, there also is a great tool that Google provides to hotlink Google Analytics data with

Google Sheets. It will automatically refresh the data on a regular basis.

You can add a column in the spreadsheet for cost for each source that you care about. You also can add a formula to compute the value of the customers you acquired. Determine the lifetime value of a customer, then multiply that by how many customers you gain to compute the total value of the customers you have acquired. Then simply compare costs to total customer value to figure out which sources are working best for you. By the way, this is a concept we plan to explore in greater detail in a book to be published in the future.

Important: One minor wrinkle is that Google Analytics has a column that says what percentage of your sessions are from new customers. However, that column can be very inaccurate for this type of calculation. For that reason, you should instead rely on data from your CRM or other back end database to determine whether your conversions are from new customers or repeat customers. Otherwise, when you do the calculation above, you will be counting repeat customers as new customers.

A major word of caution is in order at this point. Many people who calculate ROAS are so excited about it that they start thinking that the data is accurate down to 4 decimal places. The more you know about how Google Analytics and other web analytics tools work, the more you realize that there is a pretty big margin of error. For example, Google Analytics often undercounts most conversion events by about 15%. This is a known issue with web analytics programs; they often under-count actions on your site because these tools require JavaScript to successfully fire before the customer moves on to the next page.

Additionally, there are lots of cases where people are touched by multiple marketing programs, and Google Analytics by default only reports on the last marketing source. This means that multiple channels might have contributed to a conversion, but Google Analytics only credits the final channel. Furthermore, some sources are ones that are not tracked by Google Analytics, as we have talked about in prior chapters. If someone listens to a podcast, views a video ad in YouTube without taking further action, or sees an ad in Facebook but doesn't click on it, Google Analytics has nothing to record.

Said another way, a lot of things can go wrong with tracking which marketing sources are driving your conversions, but luckily, all your marketing sources will be measured the same way. There are cases when some sources are more impacted than others, but usually, the similarities are greater than the differences. For these reasons, you want to focus on the relative performance of your marketing sources and campaigns more than the absolute performance. Take all your marketing sources and campaigns and rank order them using return on ad spend. Then cut off the bottom ones and funnel that money to the ones at the top. Then figure out how to improve the ones in the middle. Don't lose sleep over what the exact ROI is for a given marketing source — you are trying to achieve a level of precision that isn't there.

We strongly encourage you to rerun these numbers on a regular cadence. You will have to figure out what cadence works for you, but you probably don't want to go longer than once a month. Facebook, Google search, YouTube, etc., all effectively work as auctions. For a given set of targeting, you get the inventory if you bid high enough. Both supply and demand are highly dynamic, so the prices can vary over time. If a lot of major advertisers decide they want to bid on the same targeting criteria as you are using, you will see ad or click prices shift. Sometimes these changes are seasonal in nature, and sometimes they are part of a long-term shift. Put simply: Do not just set it and forget it. Watch and adjust; otherwise, you might overpay for ads or miss out on ad opportunities.

Because the pricing on most ad platforms is driven by supply and demand, it can be advantageous to get in early and get out when things start to get overbid. The only way to know where you are in that cycle is to keep measuring your return on ad spend, as we covered earlier.

Assembling Your Winning Customer Acquisition Team

As you probably have gotten the sense, online marketing moves quickly, but also gets very complicated. As well, you need a mix of analytic and creative types. Hence, it requires a tricky mix of talent on your team that generally breaks down into three broad categories.

The Growth Hacker:

It seems like every week there is some hot new site or app out there, many of which allow you to advertise your product. Similarly, core online marketing techniques keep changing. Social media is very different from what it was a few years ago, and even email marketing continues to evolve. As such, you will want to staff your team with generalists who are very quick learners. You want people who are passionate about online marketing, constantly tracking the industry to see what is new. Ask people how they stay abreast of what is happening in the industry. If they aren't following key influencers, reading key blogs and newsletters every day, etc., they probably are not for you.

In order to learn all the new skills, they cannot be afraid of technology — they need to be willing to really dive in. Are they the type who will sit down with a new product and just wrestle through, using Google and YouTube to find solutions when they get stuck? If so, that is promising. Ideally, the person has a reasonable technical background (e.g., they took a computer science class or two in college), because some of these topics can get pretty technical. However, this skill can be taught; don't pass on a person who is promising, but don't hire someone who is technically illiterate.

In addition, they need to be analytical thinkers. The process we have laid out in this book requires people to test, measure, learn, and repeat. That requires someone who can review the numbers and make sense of them, especially when the data is cloudy or incomplete.

Because analysis is so fundamental to what you will be doing, this quick-learning, analytical type will likely be a full-time hire. These skills are core to your business and you cannot afford to have someone who is coming and going. You need someone who is tracking what is working and what is not on a weekly, or even daily, basis. A common job title for this type of person is "growth hacker," but you can also go with a more traditional marketing title like "online marketing manager."

Creative Types:

Another skillset you will need on the team is content creation. You will need to create digital and print ads, videos, emails, etc. That requires a mix of writers, visual designers, video specialists, and all-around creative talent. In the early days, you might have been able to get by with outsourced visual designers and copywriters, but nowadays, you will likely want to bring one or both skillsets onboard full time as you ramp up. The more aggressive your acquisition goals, the more content you will need to create. If you are running a lot of advertising programs, you will find that you can easily keep one or more writers and designers busy full time.

As an alternative, find a creative agency that you work well with, and use them consistently. This is especially beneficial to smaller companies that might not have room on their payroll for a creative team, benefits, and so on. The key is to manage the agency diligently. You are not their only client, so be proactive in communicating your goals, reviewing their work, and challenging them.

Specialists:

All the customer acquisition techniques described in the second part of the book require deep knowledge of specific techniques. For example, SEO is a topic that very quickly gets incredibly complex. If you are going to do more than dabble in SEO, you need someone who is an SEO guru. Similarly, paid search is an art unto itself. Facebook advertising can get very complicated. The same could be true of YouTube, affiliate marketing, and virtually all the techniques discussed earlier.

Furthermore, in many cases, you often can run into bugs or other issues that require the assistance of the company running the ad network. We have firsthand experience here; we've encountered issues on paid search that required contacting Google's paid search division more often than you'd think. Alternately, the targeting on YouTube didn't work as expected, so we needed to contact the YouTube experts at Google, and Facebook's audience building didn't work as advertised, so assistance was required. Google, Facebook, and the major ad platforms are better set up to support large customers and ad agencies than small, individual clients.

These issues present you with two challenges. First, if you had in-house specialists in many of these techniques, you would need a lot of specialists. It is very hard to be a guru at a number of these platforms at one time. These require too much training. Can you afford to have one SEO expert, one Facebook expert, one paid search expert, one affiliate marketing expert, etc.?

Also, you often learn how these platforms work by being able to run ads across multiple customers. If you are running ad campaigns on a given platform for a dozen, or several dozen, or many hundreds of clients, you really get to know how that platform works. It simply is hard to have that same level of knowledge if you are only supporting one company.

The second challenge, as mentioned above, is that small companies often have a tough time getting support from Google, Facebook, and the other ad platform vendors. On the other hand, the agencies tend to have close relationships with Google, Facebook, etc. and can pick up the phone and get a resolution when you run into trouble. They also often have access to early betas of new targeting functionality that can greatly increase your efficiency. We have seen early betas save customers tens of thousands, or hundreds of thousands of dollars just during the beta period.

Because of these challenges, it often makes sense to hire agencies or consultants to fill the role of specialists, managing the day-to-day responsibilities of SEO, paid search, YouTube, Facebook, and so on. You get a lot of expertise while not having to bring on board full-time people.

Having said that, the word "agency" often conjures up bad imagery for a lot of folks. They think of organizations that charge high prices and are not really that committed to your business. While that certainly can be very true, there are many agencies and consultants who are excellent.

Part of the challenge is that many agencies charge a fee based on how much you spend on media. Therefore, they are incented to have you spend more on whatever type of media they manage, regardless of the ROAS from that spend.

When interviewing agencies and consultants, let them know right up front that you will be watching the ROAS very closely. Explain your process (that you learned in this book) and your cadence for reviewing the ROAS. Really push them to understand how they think about ROAS and let them know that if ROAS is poor, you will find another firm or just cut that marketing source all together. If they have a performance mindset, they will respect your approach and will work hard to ensure that you succeed.

You might want to look at smaller agencies or even 1- or 2-person consulting shops. The smaller firms often are more set up to support this type of performance mindset. On the other hand, these smaller firms often do not have the same kind of relationships with Google, Facebook, etc. as the larger firms. Google has been known to have their reps set up on-site office hours at the major agencies to ensure they get the support they need.

If you interview a range of consultants and agencies, and ask them about their approach to ROAS, and their relationship with the ad platform vendor in question, you will usually find the right specialists for you.

Part V: Tools & Technical Considerations

A Note on Google Analytics

Throughout the book, we have talked about using web and mobile tracking tools. While there are a number of tools out there for measuring how your customers use your site or app, we are big fans of Google Analytics. First and foremost, the basic Google Analytics product is free. The product does limit you to a certain amount of data that you can collect each year. However, that limit is extremely high. If you start hitting that limit, chances are that you have built a large and very successful business.

Second, the free version is highly capable. While the paid version adds a few additional features, the free version is almost always adequate for small businesses. The amount you can track in the free version is pretty stunning once you know how to use the product. You can track virtually any action on your website or app, create custom fields that track information specific to your business, and slice and dice the data an almost infinite number of ways. There is a common saying with Google Analytics that if you cannot track something, you just don't know the product well enough. Said another way, you can customize Google Analytics to track just about anything.

Perhaps most important to you is that the product is very easy for beginners to learn. It has a number of standard reports that are very powerful, and yet fairly intuitive. Over time, you can invest more time and go deeper into the product in small increments. A good book for getting started is *Advanced Web Metrics with Google Analytics* by Brian Clifton.

If you feel more comfortable working with your data in a spreadsheet, there is a nice connector that pulls Google Analytics data into Google Sheets automatically. That allows you to perform additional calculations on your data, or combine the Google Analytics data with other data from your business.

One huge advantage to using Google Analytics is that it is widely used. It is very easy to find people who know how to use Google Analytics. Plus, any skills you acquire about Google Analytics are highly transferrable to other businesses.

Google Analytics can be used for websites and mobile apps. While you do have to purchase the paid version to combine web and mobile data together, it is a huge advantage to be able to learn one platform that can track both mobile and web.

A Plug for Tag Management— Making You More Efficient

If your online business is heavily reliant on your site (as opposed to being strictly app-based), we strongly encourage you to implement a tag management system, if at all possible. First, a little background on tags. If you implement Google Analytics, you will need to implement some code on every page of your site. If you want to implement retargeting, you again will need to place a snippet of code across your site. If you want to have Google AdWords automatically run the best converting ads, you will need to implement some conversion tracking code. In other words, in the online marketing world, there are a lot of snippets of tracking code that regularly need to get implemented. To complicate matters, the code changes from time to time, so you need to be prepared to update a given snippet to the latest spec.

The old approach to implementing these snippets of code was to insert them into your HTML, preferably in some sort of template file that was being used across your site. However, this had a lot of issues. First, as a marketing person, you had very little visibility into what tags were running. If you had a solid grasp of HTML, you could do some investigation, but it wasn't easy. Even if you looked at the HTML for a given page, it was sometimes hard to tell what code was doing what unless the code was well-documented.

The next issue is that each snippet needs to run in different places on your site. Google Analytics code runs everywhere. Your retargeting code might only run on part of your site. Your AdWords conversion tracking code only runs on the post-conversion page. Ideally, the tracking code would be in templates so the designers or developers didn't have to manually touch hundreds or thousands of pages. However, sometimes the templates that cut across the site didn't line up particularly well with where you needed certain code to run. This all resulted in a very manual and error-prone process of trying to ensure that the right code ran in the right places.

On a related note, putting the code on the page can have big implications if something goes wrong. If you insert a new snippet of code improperly, it could break other tracking code, or even worse, break your site.

Lastly and perhaps most importantly, manually inserting tracking code means that you, the marketing person, have no control. You have to go through designers and developers who often have long queues of things to do. It is not uncommon to add and modify tags every week. If you have to wait for designers or developers to get to your tracking code, things can fall seriously behind.

A tag management system resolves all of these issues by giving you a lot more control and visibility into what tags run where. You generally have a nice clean list of which tags are running, with a clean description of each one. You can easily update a given tag or insert a new tag at any time.

For a given tag, you typically have a list of rules for when it fires. For example, you can say which pages or events trigger the tag to fire. This gives you a lot of control to run a given piece of code on one page, a set of pages, or your entire site, as well as the ability to change those rules at any time.

To ensure reliability, tag managers do a number of things. First, they typically run the tags asynchronously. This means that if a piece of code runs into trouble, it should not block other code or the page itself from loading.

Another important thing the tag managers do is have wizards to help you turn on the more popular types of tracking code. You typically enter a couple key pieces of data and the tag manager will build the code. This greatly reduces the risk of errors.

Even if you are not using the wizards, the tag manager typically will run some checks on your tracking code. Before you even turn it live, the tag manager will tell you if it notices any issues with it.

Lastly, because tag managers are much easier to use than HTML, implementation of new tags is much faster. Many organizations will allow marketing professionals to create and publish their own tags. Others will allow the marketing professionals to create the tags but insist on someone reviewing them before they go live. Either way, the process is much faster than editing HTML, especially since the risk is so much lower due to the checks and balances described above.

While tag managers do exist for mobile apps, it is still

the early pioneer days of tag management for mobile apps. On the web, the benefits of tag management are huge. For mobile apps, the benefits are more modest, although the area is changing quickly.

Getting Started with Tag Management

To get a tag management system set up your on your site, you just need to add — you guessed it — a snippet of code on each page of your site. That code calls the tag management system, which in turn loads whichever snippets are supposed to fire on that specific page of your site. Your typical web designer can add this tag management code snippet to your site in a jiffy.

Once the tag management code is set up, you then go into the tag manager and enter tags that you want to run. For each tag, you will tell it which pages (or sets of pages) you want it to run on. That's it!

Don't Get Too Focused on the Last Click—A Word on Attribution Tracking

If a user clicks on ads that you show on multiple platforms, Google Analytics by default only gives credit to the last ad a user clicked. In other words, Google Analytics uses a last click attribution model. On the surface, this might not seem like a huge issue, but it can distort your data under certain situations.

If you have a product that requires a lot research and consideration, there are more chances for users to come back to your site through different paths. By contrast, impulse purchases and decisions generally are easier to track because the user often makes the decision to convert (or not) on their first visit.

One of the more common situations when this becomes a problem is when users click on ads to check out your site but don't convert until they come back a second time, often through search. This second visit often comes through branded search terms. The customer thought about the purchase and decided to go ahead, coming back by visiting a search engine and entering your brand name as the search string. Google Analytics would by default give credit to search, specifically branded search, for this conversion. However, it was the initial ad that really drove this purchase.

Another common situation is when a user clicks on

an ad, does some research on your site, but doesn't convert until they get an email from you (perhaps with a special offer) that causes them to convert. In this case, the conversion is attributed to email (assuming you are tracking your emails properly).

There are a variety of attribution models out there, including first click, last click, or linear (i.e., splitting credit across everything they clicked on). It is another complex topic that people study in depth, and there is no one attribution model that fits all businesses. However, if you are using Google Analytics, it is easy to quickly get a sense of whether you need to really focus on what attribution model you use. If you go to Conversions → Attribution, you should see a model comparison report. This allows you to see your conversions by source (or a couple other groupings) using various attribution models. If the numbers change a lot when you pick an attribution model other than last click, you probably want to pay more attention to this issue.

You can also go to Multi-Channel Funnels → Overview to see a Venn diagram of how many conversions are coming through multiple channels. The Assisted Conversions report shows last click conversions and conversions where that source played a part, but was not the last click. Lastly, you can look at the Top Conversion Paths report to see what paths (i.e., sources) users most often came through to your site. You might be surprised by how many users saw your ads on very different platforms.

A few additional caveats are in order. First, if a user

clears their cookies or visits your site from multiple devices, they will, by default, be considered different users in Google Analytics, and you won't have an accurate path to conversion in Google Analytics. There are ways to work around those issues, but that is beyond the scope of this book.

Also, if a user clicks on an ad and then later returns to your site by directly keying in your URL, Google Analytics does not overwrite the original source. Direct traffic does not count as a last click, unless there are no prior visits to your site.

In addition, if you redirect your user to a third-party site at any point in their visit, that too can throw off the attribution tracking. There are ways to deal with this. A solid Google Analytics guide like Brian Clifton's book (referenced earlier), will cover how to resolve this.

Lastly, it is important to note that Google Analytics and most web analytics platforms only track click conversions. In other words, they track when users click through an ad and ultimately convert. They do not track view-through conversions, which are cases where a user saw an ad and was influenced by it, but never clicked on it. There are dedicated attribution tracking platforms that track these view-through conversions, but they can be expensive and complex to implement. As well, they generally only work with certain ad platforms. If you are running ads on platforms that they don't work with, the value of these solutions can be greatly diminished.

Picking the Best Tools for You

In this book, we mention quite a few vendors, mostly so you have an example of who we are thinking of. Please know that we haven't been paid by any of these vendors (believe us, it's true!), nor are they sending us any nice Christmas presents. It matters less which vendor you use than that you use someone to do each of the things we have mentioned.

We tried to mention some of the popular vendors in each space, but this book is not meant to be a comprehensive vendor review. Such a review would almost certainly be out of date by the time this book is published due to how fast digital marketing is moving. Our goal is more to introduce you to these concepts than to help you try to decide which vendor is right for you. After all, the most important part about picking a vendor is understanding your own needs. That is something you will need to do.

Big Finish

We sincerely thank you for taking the time to read this book, and hope that it has helped get the wheels turning for you in terms of growing your business through customer acquisition.

So … what now? Well, that's up to you. Here is a basic list of next steps:

1. Build your foundation. Define your goals, and define what success is in terms of your customer acquisition. Is it X number of users, $X in revenues?
2. Understand your funnel — what needs to happen to achieve success defined in step 1?
3. Implement as many strategies as you can, based on budget, time, resources, and what makes the most sense for your business.
4. Test, adjust, and repeat! This is ongoing. Measure your ROAS for each strategy or channel you implement. Cut funding from lower performing channels and move that money into top performing channels, and evaluate whether you can improve middle performing channels. Pay attention to changing trends in your business as you grow, and adjust your strategies as you scale. Different strategies can work better for larger user bases versus smaller, and so on.
5. Don't get lazy. Find your groove in terms of what is working, but never assume you've peaked. There are always improvements to be made, and the world of customer acquisition changes all the time. Implement new tools and strategies as applicable.

6. Go snowboarding. Practice yoga. Play an instrument. Read. Watch TV. Do whatever relaxes you, because we all need to recharge. Then, hit the ground running!

OK, that does it. We wish you nothing but the best, and encourage you to find us on our website, www.first-millioncustomers.com, to let us know what questions, comments, or experiences you have with this material. Rome wasn't built in a day, and neither are most successful businesses. Be patient, be resilient, and be adaptable.

Ready? Set? Go!

— Ken and Chris, 2017

48815062R00083

Made in the USA
San Bernardino, CA
05 May 2017